Madonna

Titles in the People in the News series include:

PEOPLE
IN THE NEWS

Madonna

by Andy Koopmans

LUCENT
BOOKS ®

THOMSON
™
GALE

San Diego • Detroit • New York • San Francisco • Cleveland
New Haven, Conn. • Waterville, Maine • London • Munich

© 2003 by Lucent Books. Lucent Books is an imprint of The Gale Group, Inc.,
a division of Thomson Learning, Inc.

Lucent Books® and Thomson Learning™ are trademarks used herein under license.

For more information, contact
Lucent Books
27500 Drake Rd.
Farmington Hills, MI 48331-3535
Or you can visit our Internet site at http://www.gale.com

LIBRARY OF CONGRESS CATALOGING-IN-PUBLICATION DATA

Koopmans, Andy.
    Madonna / by Andy Koopmans.
        p.   cm. — (People in the news)
Includes bibliographical references (p. and index).
Summary: Profiles the early life, career goals, scandals, music, marriages, divorces,
movies, troubles, and continued success of Madonna.
    ISBN 1-59018-138-7 (hardback : alk. paper)
    1. Madonna, 1958—Juvenile literature. 2. Singers—United States—Biography—
Juvenile literature. [1. Madonna, 1958– 2. Singers. 3. Rock music. 4. Women—
Biography.] I. Title. II. People in the news (San Diego, Calif.)
    ML3930 .M26 K6 2003
    785.42166'092—dc21

                                                                2002004442

Printed in the United States of America

Table of Contents

Foreword

FAME AND CELEBRITY are alluring. People are drawn to those who walk in fame's spotlight, whether they are known for great accomplishments or for notorious deeds. The lives of the famous pique public interest and attract attention, perhaps because their experiences seem in some ways so different from, yet in other ways so similar to, our own.

Newspapers, magazines, and television regularly capitalize on this fascination with celebrity by running profiles of famous people. For example, television programs such as *Entertainment Tonight* devote all of their programming to stories about entertainment and entertainers. Magazines such as *People* fill their pages with stories of the private lives of famous people. Even newspapers, newsmagazines, and television news frequently delve into the lives of well-known personalities. Despite the number of articles and programs, few provide more than a superficial glimpse at their subjects.

Lucent's People in the News series offers young readers a deeper look into the lives of today's newsmakers, the influences that have shaped them, and the impact they have had in their fields of endeavor and on other people's lives. The subjects of the series hail from many disciplines and walks of life. They include authors, musicians, athletes, political leaders, entertainers, entrepreneurs, and others who have made a mark on modern life and who, in many cases, will continue to do so for years to come.

These biographies are more than factual chronicles. Each book emphasizes the contributions, accomplishments, or deeds that have brought fame or notoriety to the individual and shows how that person has influenced modern life. Authors portray their subjects in a realistic, unsentimental light. For example, Bill Gates—the cofounder and chief executive officer of the software giant Microsoft—has been instrumental in making personal computers the most vital tool of the modern age. Few dispute his business savvy, his perseverance, or his technical expertise, yet critics say he is ruthless in his dealings with competitors and driven more by his desire to maintain Microsoft's dominance in the computer industry than by an interest in furthering technology.

In these books, young readers will encounter inspiring stories about real people who achieved success despite enormous obstacles. Oprah Winfrey—the most powerful, most watched, and wealthiest woman on television today—spent the first six years of her life in the care of her grandparents while her unwed mother sought work and a better life elsewhere. Her adolescence was colored by promiscuity, pregnancy at age fourteen, rape, and sexual abuse.

Each author documents and supports his or her work with an array of primary and secondary source quotations taken from diaries, letters, speeches, and interviews. All quotes are footnoted to show readers exactly how and where biographers derive their information and provide guidance for further research. The quotations enliven the text by giving readers eyewitness views of the life and accomplishments of each person covered in the People in the News series.

In addition, each book in the series includes photographs, annotated bibliographies, timelines, and comprehensive indexes. For both the casual reader and the student researcher, the People in the News series offers insight into the lives of today's newsmakers—people who shape the way we live, work, and play in the modern age.

The Phenomenon

Sɪɴᴄᴇ ʜᴇʀ ꜰɪʀꜱᴛ single, "Everybody," was released in 1983, Madonna Louise Ciccone—known to the world as Madonna— has become one of the most influential and powerful figures in the entertainment industry. She also remains the most popular female solo artist in history, with twenty-two gold albums, nine platinum albums, and twenty multiplatinum albums.

In addition to being a successful performer, Madonna is a cultural obsession. She is continually analyzed and discussed by critics, journalists, academics, and fans alike. A media icon, she appears often in magazine or newspaper articles, even when she is not working. She has hundreds of websites devoted to her and dozens of fan clubs worldwide. Many universities even offer courses on Madonna, discussing both her work and her personal life.

Few celebrities have garnered as much media attention with their personal lives as Madonna has. As journalist Jancee Dunn writes, it is hard not to be intrigued by Madonna: "Show me a person who is uninterested in Madonna and I'll show you a liar." [1]

Madonna has used her public appeal to become a wealthy woman. She is a shrewd and successful businessperson with an estimated fortune of more than $100 million. Throughout her career, she has retained tight control on her business matters. And she has built a media empire with several companies of her own, including her prominent record label, Maverick, through which she has helped launch and advance the careers of numerous other musicians.

Madonna achieved her wealth and celebrity through discipline, talent, and perseverance. After spending twenty years as

Madonna is the most successful female solo entertainer in history.

an entertainer, Madonna remains a serious artist, who still searches for new ways to intrigue audiences and to challenge herself. "I never want to repeat myself," she said in 2001. "I don't see the point [of performing] unless you offer something that is going to boggle the senses."[2]

Chapter 1

Getting Attention

MADONNA LOUISE CICCONE was born August 16, 1958, at Bay City Mercy Hospital in Bay City, Michigan. She was the third of six children and the first daughter of Silvio "Tony" Ciccone and Madonna Fortin Ciccone. Growing up in a large family, where she had to compete with her siblings for the attention of her parents, Madonna developed a strong personality and work ethic. She also discovered and honed her natural talent for performance. These qualities became the foundation for her life as a persistent, bold, and successful performer.

Origins

A first-generation American, Tony Ciccone's known genealogical roots date back to 1867, when his grandfather was born in the Abruzzi province of Pacentro, Italy. His parents, Gaetano and Michelina Ciccone, immigrated to the United States in 1920, settling near Pittsburgh, Pennsylvania. Gaetano spent the rest of his life working in steel mills, while Michelina raised their six children, all boys.

Tony, the youngest, was an aggressive boy who worked hard. He saw the economic opportunity that education could provide in America and became the only one of Gaetano and Michelina's children to graduate from college.

While serving in the U.S. Air Force, Tony Ciccone attended the wedding of one of his best friends. There, he met the groom's sister, a French Canadian woman named Madonna Fortin. Soon after they met, Ciccone proposed marriage.

The couple married in 1955 at Bay City's Catholic Visitation Church. They settled in Pontiac, Michigan, twenty-five miles north of Detroit, where Ciccone had a job as an engineer for the Chrysler Corporation. In May 1956 and August 1957, Madonna Fortin gave birth to their first two children, Anthony and Martin. Then, in 1958, during a visit with relatives in Bay City, Madonna Fortin went into labor with her third child. On August 16, she delivered the Ciccones' first daughter, whom she and her husband named Madonna Louise and nicknamed Little Nonnie.

Standing Out

Tony Ciccone and Madonna Sr. had three more children in the early 1960s: Paula, Christopher, and Melanie. Because the family

Madonna with her younger brother, Christopher Ciccone (left). Madonna was the third of six children born to Tony and Madonna Fortin Ciccone.

became so large, the younger Madonna had to struggle to stand out from the rest of the kids. To win attention from her parents, she learned early on how to perform and entertain her family. For instance, she often jumped onto a tabletop and imitated Shirley Temple, doing a tap dance to the delight of her parents.

Madonna developed a love for being the family's center of attention. Sometimes, however, this annoyed her siblings. According to her brother Christopher:

> She was spoiled from the very beginning. She was the oldest girl, and was considered our parents' favorite. That, combined with the fact that she was really aggressive and wanted her way, and got it, made her a spoiled kid. But she was good-hearted. She liked to take care of the bunch. She was also very bossy.[3]

Madonna agrees, saying, "I always thought that I should be treated like a star when I was a kid. [I always wanted] the biggest piece of the cake. Y'know, stuff like that."[4]

Madonna also worked hard at school to win the favor of her parents. Ciccone and Madonna Sr. raised their children in a strict Catholic household, where church attendance, hard work, and good grades were demanded. Madonna says, "My father brought me up to be very goal-oriented—to be a lawyer or doctor and study, study, study."[5]

Throughout her school years, Madonna worked hard at school and usually got the best grades of all the Ciccone children. She recalls:

> I was a very good student. I got all A's. My father rewarded us for good grades. He gave us quarters and fifty-cent pieces for every A we got. I was really competitive, and my brothers and sisters hated me for it. I made the most money off of every report card.[6]

Losing Her Mother

As a child, Madonna was very close to her mother. Since they shared the same name, Madonna felt they had a special bond, and she often slept with her parents to be near her mother.

Tony Ciccone was the disciplinarian, and Madonna remembers her mother as a gentle, loving woman who was good to her family. Madonna Sr. was so permissive and gentle with her children that young Madonna often misbehaved on purpose, knowing her mother would not do anything about it. Madonna recalls:

Growing Up Catholic

Madonna grew up in a strict Catholic household. In a 1985 *Time* magazine article entitled "Now: Madonna on Madonna," written by Denise Worrell, Madonna reflects on her religious upbringing:

Catholicism gives you a strength, an inner strength, whether you end up believing it later or not. It's the backbone. I think maybe the essence of Catholicism I haven't rejected, but the theory of it, I have, if that makes any sense. I don't go to church but I believe in God. I don't say my rosary but I think about things like that. The thing that has remained with me most, I guess, is the idea that you do unto others as they do unto you. It's not right to steal or lie or cheat. I think it's pretty creepy when guys cheat on their wives and the other way around, stuff like that. When I was little, I had all the usual feelings of guilt. I was very conscious of God watching everything I did.

Madonna was raised in a stern Catholic environment.

I have a lot of feelings of love and warmth for her but sometimes I think I tortured her. I think little kids do that to people who are really good to them. They can't believe they're not getting yelled at or something so they taunt you, and I really taunted my mother.[7]

In 1962, when Madonna was four years old, her mother was diagnosed with breast cancer. Madonna Sr. became fragile and weak and could no longer play with her children. Madonna did not understand the change in her mother and became angry with her. Madonna recalls:

I remember she was really sick and was sitting on the couch. . . . I remember climbing up on her back and saying, "Play with me, play with me," and she wouldn't. She couldn't and she started crying and I got really angry with her and I remember, like, pounding on her back with my fist and saying, "Why are you doing this?" Then I realized she was crying. . . . I remember feeling stronger than she was. I was so little and I put my arms around her and I could feel her body underneath me sobbing and I felt like she was the child. I stopped tormenting her after that.[8]

After a year-long hospitalization, Madonna Sr. died from complications from the cancer. Not wanting to show her pain

I Wished I Was Black

In a March 23, 1989, *Rolling Stone* magazine article entitled "Madonna: The *Rolling Stone* Interview," Madonna told writer Bill Zehme that living in a predominantly black neighborhood during her early childhood had an influence on her self-image.

When I was a little girl, I wished I was black. All my girlfriends were black. I was living in Pontiac, Michigan, and [because I was white] I was definitely the minority in the neighborhood. White people were scarce there. All my friends were black. I was incredibly jealous of all my black girlfriends because they could have braids in their hair that stuck up everywhere. So, I would go through this incredible ordeal of putting wire in my hair and braiding it so that I could make my hair stick up. I used to make cornrows and everything.

and distress to her children who watched at her bedside, she or-
dered a hamburger from the hospital cafeteria as her dinner the
night she died.

Taking Her Mother's Role

Tony Ciccone was devastated by his wife's death. Unable to
cope alone with the loss and the large family, he sent several of
his children to live with relatives. Madonna, however, stayed
home to take care of him.

With her mother gone, Madonna desired her father's affec-
tion more than ever. One way she kept her father's attention was
by taking over her mother's role as much as possible. She did
most of the household chores and helped to cook and take care of
the other children—even though she was only five years old. "I really felt like I was the main female of the house," she remembers.
"There was no woman between [me and my father], no mother."[9]

Stepmother

After a few weeks, Ciccone hired a housekeeper, and the children staying with relatives were able to come home again. But
the Ciccone children were too wild and rambunctious for the
housekeeper and she quit, as did several of her successors. The
one housekeeper who stayed was named Joan Gustafson. She
and Ciccone eventually fell in love, and in 1966, they married.

Madonna was unhappy, though, and jealous of her new
stepmother. She did not like having to share her father's attention. Additionally, Joan's strict and serious personality was a big
change from Madonna Sr.'s warm, kind temperament.

Even with her new stepmother in charge, Madonna continued to bear a large responsibility for taking care of the other children; this included the two that Joan gave birth to in the two
years following her wedding to Ciccone. Madonna remembers:
"I was the oldest girl and always got stuck with the main housekeeping chores. . . . I was forced to grow up fast. . . . I really saw
myself as a Cinderella with a wicked stepmother."[10]

Madonna also resented the fact that, in order to save money,
her stepmother made identical dresses for the four Ciccone sisters out of the same bolt of cloth. Madonna wanted to stand out

Madonna's sister,
Melanie, at the
christening of
Madonna's son,
Rocco.

and be different, and she felt stripped of her individuality by having to wear the same clothes as her siblings. She recalls: "She would sew the exact same . . . dress pattern for me and my three sisters. I detested that—looking like my sisters. I wanted to be my own person."[11]

Madonna soon learned to assert her individuality by thinking of ways to change her clothes. She turned them inside out or ripped them in an effort to show that she was different from her sisters.

Acting Out

In 1968, when Madonna was ten, the Ciccones moved from Pontiac, Michigan, to Rochester Hills, an affluent suburb of Detroit. There, Madonna attended St. Andrews Catholic School and then went on to public school, eventually attending Adams High School.

During these adolescent years, Madonna was unhappy at home. Her new stepmother made her miserable, and she still felt the loss of her mother's attention. So she sought the attention she needed outside her family. She says, "I . . . turned my need on to the world and said, 'Okay, I don't have a mother to love me, I'm going to make the world love me.'"[12]

A natural performer, Madonna began her quest to make the world love her by entering talent contests at school. These performances allowed her to be creative and also allowed her to be in control, something she felt she had lost in her home life. She recalls:

> Talent shows were . . . my one chance a year to be who I wanted and to show people who I was. It gave me the chance to do something with my energy, because I would conceptualize it, plan the costumes, plan everything. I would try to get other girls involved so I could tell everybody what to do and push them around. . . . I've always been a control freak. I'm uncomfortable when I'm not in charge.[13]

In 1968, Madonna and her family moved to this home in Rochester Hills, Michigan.

This sense of control over her work was something she would take with her into her adult career.

So too were her boldness and love of shocking audiences. Even during her earliest Shirley Temple tap-dance imitations on tabletops at home, she liked shocking people—Madonna ended those dances by lifting her skirt and flashing her underwear. And at her fifth-grade talent contest, she alarmed her father by performing a go-go dance in a tiny bikini with her skin painted fluorescent green.

These performances and many others earned Madonna a great deal of attention. She loved the spotlight and applause of an audience. Influenced by her love of performance, Madonna dreamed of being an actress like the glamorous 1940s and 1950s movie stars she admired, among them Bette Davis, Jean Harlow, and especially Marilyn Monroe. In high school, she became in-

As a teenager, Madonna (center) participated in school talent shows and plays.

volved in the theater department and appeared in numerous productions. She had a strong stage presence, and many of her teachers thought she would be famous one day. Beverly Gibson, her drama teacher, recalls: "When the spotlight came on her, she was pure magic. . . . I would watch her on stage with that vibrant personality and charisma and think to myself, 'Oh, my, it is inevitable, isn't it?'"[14]

Dating

During her high school years, Madonna also began dating. She was forward and aggressive, approaching boys she liked and letting them know she wanted to go out with them. But her attitude was misunderstood by others and gave her a reputation of being promiscuous.

Madonna was upset about her reputation because she never thought it fit her. She thought it was natural to be strong and direct if she liked a boy. She says:

> I remember liking boys and not feeling inhibited. I never played little games; if I liked a boy, I'd confront him. . . . But when you're that aggressive . . . the boys get the wrong impression of you. They mistake your forwardness for sexual promiscuity.[15]

A Mentor

Even though she was dating, Madonna continued to excel in her studies and extracurricular activities. The strong work ethic her father instilled in her caused her to push herself. She was never content to relax in her accomplishments or rest at her level of talent or achievement.

She applied this work ethic and discipline when she took up dance in high school. In ninth grade, Madonna joined the high school jazz dance class, but she found it too easy. Rather than stay in the class, she quit, deciding instead to try ballet, which she thought would be more challenging. She became friends with a classmate who was a serious ballet dancer and who introduced her to dance teacher Christopher Flynn.

*A born performer, Madonna (center) naturally took to such
extracurricular activities as dance and cheerleading.*

In his mid-forties when Madonna first came to his class at
the Rochester School of Ballet, Flynn was a strict taskmaster who
worked his students very hard. Madonna liked the challenge
and difficulty of Flynn's class, and she dedicated hours each day
to practice. She was rewarded with Flynn's recognition and respect. She recalls:

> I was with these really professional ballet dancers. I had
> only studied jazz up to then, so I had to work twice as
> hard as anybody else and Christopher Flynn was im-
> pressed with me. He saw . . . how hard I worked.[16]

Madonna and Flynn also became friends. Madonna had
never felt like she fit in with her peer group; instead, she always
felt out of place. She recalls, "I knew people were interested in
me, but they thought I was a weirdo."[17] But in Flynn, the first gay
man she had met, she found someone else who was an outsider
and who was exotic and artistic. She felt a kinship with Flynn
that she had not felt with many of her peers.

Flynn also provided important emotional support for Madonna, support she was not getting from her family. Her father saw performing as a hobby, not a serious pursuit, but Flynn encouraged Madonna and gave her the attention she craved during this period. Madonna says:

> I really loved him. He was my first taste of what I thought was an artistic person. . . . He educated me, he took me to museums and told me about art. He was my mentor, my father, my imaginative lover, my brother, everything, because he understood me.[18]

As her mentor, Flynn found Madonna to be an insatiable student. Although she was intelligent, she had not had much exposure to the fine arts and cultural history. Flynn introduced her to art history, classical music, and other areas of culture she had

In high school, Madonna began to develop as an artist but felt alienated from her peers.

never experienced. She was eager to learn as much as she could. Flynn says of her:

> Madonna was a blank page, believe me, and she wanted desperately to be filled in. She knew nothing at all about art, classical music, sculpture, fashion, civilization— nothing about life really. I mean, she was just a child. But she had a burning desire to *learn,* that girl.[19]

Transformation and Rebellion

Under Flynn's tutelage, Madonna transformed. She became a vegetarian. She no longer sought to be the center of attention at school. Instead, she was content to spend time on her own. She became serious and quiet, and her usual boisterous wisecracks and jokes disappeared. Carol Stier, a high school classmate, remembers walking into class one day during their junior year and seeing the "new" Madonna. Whereas Madonna usually wore makeup and skirts, Stier recalls:

> [She] had a bandanna with bold print wrapped around her short hair and was wearing blue jean overalls and ankle-high combat boots. She had no makeup on but was still pretty. . . . It was a big change. She no longer bothered talking to [her friends], not interested in being friends any more. During class she was quiet and studious. The wisecracks were out.[20]

Outside of school, Madonna did little more than practice dance and spend time with Flynn. In her senior year, Flynn introduced her to the gay clubs of downtown Detroit. There, Madonna first heard club music, which had a significant influence on her sound and career. She loved the pulsing dance music and the atmosphere of freedom and abandon. Flynn recalls: "She loved it. . . . She just cleared the floor and we just cut loose and everybody loved her. It's not that she was showing off, she just thoroughly enjoyed dancing and it sprang out of her."[21]

Spending time with Flynn and at the clubs was also a form of rebellion against her father. Tony Ciccone wanted to keep his

Frustrated with life in Rochester Hills, Madonna left home in 1976 to study dance at the University of Michigan.

oldest daughter safe and close to home. But Madonna became dissatisfied with her sheltered, middle-class suburban life in Rochester Hills. And her friendship with Flynn introduced her to a larger world that she was impatient to enter.

College

Madonna got the opportunity to leave Rochester Hills and venture out into the world in 1976, when she went away to college. Flynn encouraged Madonna to apply for a dance scholarship at the University of Michigan (U-M) in Ann Arbor, Michigan. Flynn had been appointed to the dance faculty at the school and wanted his star pupil and friend to come with him. Because she had accumulated so many extra credits during high school, Madonna was able to graduate in December 1975, a semester early. She spent the spring practicing and trying out for a scholarship at U-M. With Flynn's guidance and support, she was accepted into the dance program for the fall of 1976. Although Madonna's father would have preferred that she pursue a more academic major, he supported her decision to leave Rochester Hills for Ann Arbor. In September 1976, Madonna left home and moved into the dormitory on U-M campus.

While at U-M, Madonna reveled in the newfound freedom of living away from home. She spent most of her nights at clubs in Ann Arbor, dancing with her college roommate, Whitley Setrakian, and other friends. She often danced until early in the morning, sleeping only a few hours before she had to get up for ballet class. However, she was dedicated and never missed a single class.

Turning Point

In Madonna's first year at U-M, Pearl Lang came to the school as a visiting dance professor. This proved to be a turning point in Madonna's academic and dancing career. A former soloist with the prestigious Martha Graham Dance Company and the founder of the Pearl Lang School of Dance, Lang was one of the best-known dancers in the world. Although Madonna was not able to study with Lang at U-M, she was able to see her perform. Madonna was inspired by Lang's dancing abilities and became determined to dance for Lang's company one day.

Since early childhood, Madonna had dreamed of becoming a famous performer, and she was beginning to tire of school. She was a good student and got good grades, but she was less and less sure that an academic dance career was something she wanted to pursue. She wanted to be a star, not a teacher. And she thought going to New York City to study with Lang and become a professional dancer would be a faster way to realize her ambitions.

A Summer with Pearl Lang

In pursuit of this goal, Madonna went to North Carolina to audition for Pearl Lang's summer workshop at Duke University. She auditioned for the judges, Lang herself among them. After the audition, as everyone was preparing to leave, Madonna walked over to the judges' table and announced that she was from Michigan and had seen Pearl Lang's work there. Lang recalls:

She was really brassy. I recognized her right away as the
same girl who had danced so spectacularly during the audition. . . . Then she looked right at me and said that the
only way she would take the scholarship would be if she
could study with Pearl Lang. . . . I told her that I was Pearl
Lang and that she could study with me for the summer.[22]

Madonna attended the workshop during the summer of 1977.
Flynn paid for her bus fare from Detroit to Durham, North
Carolina, where the workshop was held. He also gave her enough
money to stay in the Duke University dormitory. The workshop
was exhausting but exhilarating, and dancing with Lang inspired
Madonna to continue working toward her goal of becoming a
professional dancer. When the workshop was over, Madonna approached Lang and asked for a position with her company in New
York. Lang recalls:

[Madonna] came right to the point and asked me if I
needed anyone in my New York company. I told her
that there was a possibility, but I knew she had no
money. . . . I asked how she was going to manage to get
there, find a place to live, and have enough money to
eat. Her answer was typically Madonna when she told
me not to worry about it, that she'd work it out.[23]

Dreams of New York

Madonna returned to Ann Arbor in the fall, determined to
move to New York. When she talked to Flynn about it, he told
her to go, even though she was still at least two years away from
graduating from college.

Her father and some of her college professors disagreed,
however. Tony Ciccone was a practical man who valued education and thought that his daughter should first earn her degree
before pursuing her dreams. Likewise, Madonna's college professors told her that New York City would always be there and
that her artistic abilities would be better served by staying in
school. But Madonna listened to Flynn instead.

Madonna spent the rest of her time at U-M working odd jobs
after classes to make money for her move to New York. She sold

In 1978, Madonna dropped out of college and moved to New York, hoping to become a star.

ice cream at Baskin-Robbins, worked as a waitress at a local campus bar, and posed as a nude model for life drawing classes. She also continued to spend many hours practicing dance in preparation for her career ahead.

Leaving Michigan

After saving up enough money for a plane ticket and pocket money, Madonna dropped out of U-M in 1978 at the end of the spring semester. As she left Michigan behind, Madonna embarked on an uncertain artistic career. She had spent her youth garnering the attention of her family and peers, but it was not enough. She wanted a larger audience—the world, if possible. She flew to New York with the single ambition of becoming a star. And the sooner the better.

Chapter 2

Struggle and Sacrifice

M ADONNA'S FIRST YEARS in New York were both difficult and exciting. She knew before leaving for Michigan that becoming a professional dancer was going to be hard and require struggle and sacrifice. But no matter how difficult it would be, she was determined to become a star.

In the Middle of Everything

Arriving in New York City in July 1978, Madonna recalls that she had only thirty-five dollars and a bag full of tights. She took a cab into the city and asked the driver to drop her off somewhere exciting. She recalls:

> I got in a taxi and told the driver to take me to the middle of everything. That turned out to be Times Square. . . . I got out of the cab and I was overwhelmed because the buildings are . . . really high. . . . This guy started following me around. . . . I said hi to him, and he said, "Why are you walking around with a winter coat and a suitcase?" And I said, "I just got off the plane." And then he said, "Why don't you go home and get rid of it?" And I said, "I don't live anywhere." He was dumbfounded. So he said, "Well, you can stay at my apartment." So I stayed there for the first two weeks. He didn't try . . . anything. He showed me where everything was, and he fed me breakfast. It was perfect. I relied on the kindness of strangers.[24]

Hand-to-Mouth

By late summer, Madonna found an apartment on the run-down Lower East Side of Manhattan. Her father came to visit soon

Choices

Madonna's personal life was a source of public interest and controversy throughout her career, including her admission, after her daughter Lourdes was born in 1996, that she had undergone more than one abortion during her early years in New York. Quoted in *Goddess: Inside Madonna*, by Barbara Victor, Madonna discusses her feelings about her past choices:

> You always have regrets when you make those decisions, but you have to look at your lifestyle and ask yourself, "Am I at a place in my life where I can devote a lot of time to being the really good parent I want to be? None of us wants to make mistakes in that role, and I imagine a lot of women look at the way our parents raised us and say, "I definitely wouldn't want to do it quite that way." I think you have to be mentally prepared for it. If you're not, you're only doing the world a disservice by bringing up a child you don't really want. . . . I think about it when I think that I could have a child right now who is five or even ten years old. Things happen when they're meant to happen, and if it comes along again, the chance of parenthood, and I'm ready, I'll do it. And that's all there is to that.

after she moved in, and he was concerned about her safety and health when he saw the squalid conditions. There were a lot of cockroaches in the bedroom, the entryway smelled of stale beer, and homeless people slept in the hallways at night.

Ciccone tried to convince Madonna to return to Michigan with him, but she refused. She did not mind living poor while pursuing her dreams. She says, "Living a hand-to-mouth existence didn't bother me so much. Not having a huge amount of comfort for me was [not a problem]."[25]

Dancing and Odd Jobs

Soon after arriving in New York, Madonna walked into Pearl Lang's school at Alvin Ailey American Dance Center while Lang was teaching a class. "Here I am," she said. "I made it!"[26] It had been more than a year since Madonna had studied with Lang in North Carolina, and Lang was surprised to see the girl.

Nonetheless, Lang gave Madonna the position that she had promised her, which meant Madonna would attend classes with Lang for several hours each day. Madonna also had to work to pay her living expenses. To help her, Lang arranged for her to take a part-time job at New York's Russian Tea Room restaurant as a hatcheck girl. The job did not last long. Madonna was fired after two months because she was rude to customers. She lost several other part-time jobs for the same reason.

Struggling to make enough money to pay rent and buy food, Madonna decided to return to nude modeling. She was able to find work easily as a model posing for professional photographers. Although she did not enjoy it, she found the work better than the other jobs.

Madonna also struggled with her dance career. Her first months working with Lang's company went well. She worked hard, and Lang noticed her talent, casting her in several

An early modeling photo. Fired from several jobs, Madonna turned to modeling to make ends meet.

performances. But Madonna wanted to become the company's principal solo dancer, the star performer. She was impatient for fame, not wanting to spend years as a secondary dancer in a large troupe before being recognized. Madonna also questioned whether dance was going to make her famous. Although she was a good dancer, she realized that the competition was great— there were many dancers as good as or better than she was, and her chances of becoming a star were no greater than most of the people she worked with. Realizing this, she began to lose interest in dance.

These doubts and her impatience for fame undermined her work. She and Lang had numerous arguments over small things. Madonna was unhappy and complained because she was frustrated and restless. She quit several weeks later, announcing to Lang that she was going to be a rock singer. "So, with all that promise, she gave up dancing,"[27] says Lang.

Change of Focus

Madonna's quitting dance seems a drastic change, but she recalls that she came to see dance as an impractical means of achieving her goals. She says, "I sort of got tired of [dancing] after a while, because it was very difficult and there was no money in it."[28]

She did, however, see money in music. In 1979, an old U-M friend, a drummer named Steve Bray, moved to New York, and the two worked together on ideas for songs. Even though she had no musical training and could not play any instrument, Madonna decided that music would be a faster route to success and stardom than dance.

The Patrick Hernandez Revue

After quitting Lang's school, Madonna started answering music trade magazine and newspaper advertisements for singers. In March 1979, she auditioned to be a backup singer for a European disco star, Patrick Hernandez, who was planning a world tour. Despite her inexperience, she was selected from fifteen hundred others to be a backup singer and dancer for the show.

The tour, called *The Patrick Hernandez Revue*, left for Europe in June 1979. But after her arrival in Paris, the first stop in the

A Certain Sacrifice

In the late 1970s, as Madonna's musical career was just beginning, she auditioned for parts in feature films but was turned down repeatedly. Frustrated, she began answering auditions for lower-budget films. In 1979, she won the lead role in a low-budget film called *A Certain Sacrifice*, directed by Stephen Jon Lewicki.

When it was released in 1985, *A Certain Sacrifice* caused a lot of controversy because it was very sexually explicit and violent. In her October 15, 1985, *Wall Street Journal* article, "Hotter Than Furnaces: Exposing Madonna's Maiden Film," writer Julie Salamon describes *A Certain Sacrifice* as "kind of a long MTV video with thinly developed themes of sadomasochism and ritual violence [that] follows the romance of a preppie turned street kid who falls in love with a seductress called Bruna (Madonna)."

Critics and journalists universally disliked the film, saying it was amateurish and of generally poor quality in its writing and production. Nonetheless, the video sold more than fifty thousand copies in the first week of its release. Critics said that Madonna's appearance in the film was the only reason it sold so well and that it seemed to exploit her recent stardom. The director, however, claimed that for financial reasons he had not been able to finish the film until 1985 and the timing was coincidental.

Lewicki also defended himself, saying in Salamon's article that he had a right to release his film. He claimed he had taken a risk by casting Madonna before she was famous and deserved the financial success that came afterward. According to Lewicki, "I took a chance on Madonna when she was absolutely nobody and I'm the one who put the money into the movie."

After its initial popularity, sales for *A Certain Sacrifice* dwindled. Although it is still considered a cult film by some ardent fans and collectors, most viewers consider the film a flop.

A still from A Certain Sacrifice, *Madonna's first movie appearance.*

European disco star Patrick Hernandez chose Madonna to be a backup singer in his 1979 tour, The Patrick Hernandez Revue.

tour, Madonna became unhappy with what she considered the unprofessional attitude of Hernandez and his troupe. While Madonna spent hours practicing, the others went to parties. Thus, despite the extravagant lifestyle the job offered—she was given a room in an expensive Parisian apartment, a new wardrobe, and all the lavish food and drink she liked—she was unsatisfied and miserable. Madonna's ambition was stardom, but not only for what it could buy. She wanted to perform, to be part of the creative process, and to work hard. As the weeks passed, Madonna knew that she could be achieving more. Frustrated, she quit the *revue*, borrowed plane fare from Hernandez, and flew home.

Back in New York, Madonna felt as though she were having to start over again. She was broke, a college dropout, and had quit her first two jobs as a performer soon after getting them. She felt directionless and frustrated, but she struggled against these feelings. Her ambition and determination prevailed, and not long after her return to New York, she looked again for artistic opportunities.

The Breakfast Club

In May of 1979, a few weeks before leaving for Paris, Madonna met Dan Gilroy, an aspiring musician twelve years her senior. They got along well, and when she returned to New York, they began dating. Dan and his brother Ed lived together in a large converted synagogue in a section of New York City called Queens. They were aspiring musicians who supported themselves by working part-time jobs.

Soon after they began dating, Madonna moved in with Dan Gilroy, and he taught her how to play the guitar and drums. She was surprised at her ability, and Gilroy was a good teacher, patient and encouraging. "It was one of the happiest times of my life," she recalls. "I really felt loved."[29]

She and the Gilroy brothers then decided to start a band. Madonna recruited a friend, bass player Angie Smit, into the band. By late summer, the four were practicing as a punk-rock band called the Breakfast Club, so named because they often rehearsed all night and afterward ate breakfast at a nearby Italian restaurant.

The band gave their first performance on a sidewalk in downtown New York City, playing to office workers on their lunch breaks. Soon afterward, they played in clubs around the city. Madonna wrote numerous songs for the band. A number of them were angry rock songs about alienation, but she also wrote many ballads, including one about her mother's death. Although Madonna wrote these songs, she did not sing them; instead, she played the drums.

A few months later, Smit left the band, citing personal problems, and two new members joined the Breakfast Club—Mike Monahan and Gary Burke. Monahan played drums and Burke played bass. With a new drummer in place, Madonna began playing keyboard. The performances never paid much money, and the band members worked day jobs to pay the bills.

When she was not working at various part-time jobs, Madonna spent a lot of her time promoting the band. She spent hours each day on the telephone with agents, club owners, and anyone else she could find who could schedule performances or teach her something about the music business. Dan Gilroy remembers: "She'd be up in the morning, a quick cup of coffee, then right to phone calls, calling everybody—everybody.

Madonna's first attempt at rock stardom was as songwriter and drummer for a band called the Breakfast Club.

Madonna prepares for a show. Madonna's aspirations to be a lead singer led her to form her own band, the Emmys.

Everyone from [local record dealer] Bleecker Bob's to potential management."[30]

Madonna also wanted to become the band's lead singer, feeling that it made sense because she wrote many of the songs. Monahan and Burke agreed, feeling that bands became more popular with an attractive female lead singer. But Dan and Ed Gilroy disagreed. The dispute grew, and neither Madonna nor the Gilroys would back down. Unable to compromise, the band broke up, and Madonna moved out of the synagogue. She also ended her dating relationship with Dan Gilroy, but they parted with mutual respect for each other.

Hitting Bottom

In 1980, following the breakup of the Breakfast Club, Madonna, Monahan, and Burke started a new band. They rented space in the Music Building, an old building in a dangerous New York neighborhood. The band's lineup changed several times, and Madonna struggled to keep the band going. The name was changed several times, too, finally becoming the Emmys, "*Emmy*" being one of Madonna's nicknames.

These were hard times. Madonna struggled during 1980 to make enough money to feed and shelter herself. She lived in a cheap, dirty, and cold apartment that had no shower but was around the corner from the Music Building. She also ate very little, surviving on a diet of popcorn.

One morning in January 1981, Burke found her lying on the floor of her apartment, crying. She was fully dressed, curled into a ball trying to keep warm, and suffering from the flu. Frustrated and tired, Madonna called Dan Gilroy and asked if she could move back into the synagogue for a while to get over her illness. Gilroy agreed, and over the next couple of weeks he helped nurse her back to health. With her health, Madonna also regained her strength and resolve.

Madonna went back to work, continuing her struggle to support herself and to keep the Emmys together. When she was not rehearsing with or promoting for the band, she spent time doing nude modeling for painters to make a little money. She also continued her popcorn diet when she could not scrounge a free meal from friends, and she accepted gifts of cast-off clothing and discarded makeup.

Madonna's First Agent

In the spring of 1981, Madonna secured an important performance for the Emmys at Max's Kansas City, one of the most popular music venues in New York City. She and the band rehearsed for weeks to get ready for the performance. All of her energy went into the band, and during this period Madonna often slept overnight in the Music Building's studio space, too tired to walk around the corner to go home.

One morning she met Camille Barbone, a music agent with Gotham Records, in the Music Building elevator. Madonna convinced Barbone to come and watch the Emmys rehearse and also made Barbone promise to come see them perform at Max's Kansas City. Barbone kept her promise and went to see the band

In 1981, Madonna left the Emmys and launched her solo career.

perform. Madonna was now the Emmys' lead singer and song-writer. As she performed, Barbone saw Madonna's raw talent; however, she thought the band was terrible.

Barbone offered Madonna a contract to become her agent but insisted that she leave behind the other members of the band. The contract also stated that Barbone would manage and help direct Madonna's career, provide her with a new apartment, pay her one hundred dollars a week, and find her part-time work as a house cleaner. Further, Madonna would have unlimited access to a professional studio where she could write and rehearse. Madonna agreed to the terms and signed the contract on March 17, 1981.

Sacrifices

As her contract required, Madonna left the Emmys. This disappointed the three other band members, men who had become close friends of hers, and the breakup was emotional. Gary Burke even accused Madonna of betraying the band. Madonna was sad to disappoint her friends, but she was willing to do it. She felt that she had to sacrifice personal relationships when necessary to further her career.

Madonna also sacrificed her relationship with Barbone. From March 1981 to February 1982, Barbone acted as Madonna's agent. The two also became constant companions, going shopping and seeing movies together, and even taking vacations together. But their professional relationship suffered after a few months. Barbone worked hard to promote Madonna's career, arranging steady performances and a steady income for Madonna and making it possible for Madonna to record an as-yet unreleased demo tape through Gotham Records.

Nonetheless, Madonna grew impatient again. She was tired of waiting for her big break and accused Barbone of laziness. Madonna felt she could find better representation, an agent who would move her career along faster. So she spoke with other agents without telling Barbone.

In late 1981, a representative from the William Morris Agency—a powerful agency in show business—showed interest in representing Madonna. Thrilled by the prospect, she decided to fire Barbone. Barbone was stunned, but the pair parted ways. Within a few weeks of firing Barbone, however, Madonna was notified that William Morris was not interested in representing her after all. Suddenly, she was on her own again.

Big Break

In the spring of 1982, without a band or an agent, Madonna went back to her popcorn diet and spartan existence. She moved into a friend's apartment and reunited with Steve Bray to work on new material. After a few weeks, they had enough songs to record a new demo tape. They recorded four songs and took the tape to New York City dance clubs, hoping to convince DJs to play it. One of the clubs was Danceteria, a popular New York nightspot.

Mark Kamins was the DJ at Danceteria; he was also an aspiring record producer. He and Madonna liked each other upon meeting, and they began dating. Kamins offered to use his contacts in the music industry to promote Madonna's career and to get her a record contract if she would let him produce her first album. She agreed.

Madonna poses for a publicity shot. In 1982 Madonna's first single, "Everybody," climbed to number one on the Billboard *dance chart.*

Kamins and Madonna went into the studio and rerecorded what Kamins thought was her best song, a dance tune called "Everybody." Once they completed production in early 1982, he took the record to a friend, Mike Rosenblatt. Rosenblatt worked for Sire Records, a label owned by Warner Brothers' music corporation. Rosenblatt liked the song and played it for his boss, Sire Records president Seymour Stein. Stein was so enthusiastic about the song and what Rosenblatt told him about Madonna that he insisted she come meet him. He remembers his first impressions of Madonna when she arrived: "She was anxious to make the deal. . . . She had an almost ruthless edge on her. I mean that in all the best ways. You could just tell, this woman would go far."[31]

Stein offered to pay Madonna and Kamins fifteen thousand dollars to produce two dance singles (a record with one song on each side) for Sire Records. Madonna and Kamins would have to pay for their own studio time, which would use up a lot of the money. But it was still a good opportunity because Stein said that if the two releases did well, Madonna could produce more singles—perhaps an album—through Sire Records. Madonna accepted the offer and was grateful to Kamins for arranging the deal. Inspired, she wrote the lyrics to her now-famous song "Lucky Star," dedicating it to Kamins to thank him.

In the fall of 1982, Madonna's first single, "Everybody," was released. In November 1982, it appeared on *Billboard* magazine's charts, rankings used by the music industry to determine the success or failure of a recording. Although the song did not make it into the magazine's all-important Top 100 pop chart, it did go to the number one spot on the dance chart. After years of struggle and sacrifice, Madonna had her first hit.

Chapter 3

New Beginnings

T HE SUCCESS OF Madonna's first single, "Everybody," suggested to Sire Records and Warner Brothers that Madonna was a potential star. Madonna, however, was sure of it. "Everybody" marked the new beginning of her career, and she told Kamins that she was a new person, saying: "The old me was broke. The old me had no place to live. The old me was someone my father wasn't proud of. The old me was Madonna Louise Ciccone. The new me is *Madonna*."[32]

Learning the Business

Madonna was confident about her future, and she continued to worked hard to achieve her goals. Eager to learn about the music business, she wanted to monitor and direct her career as much as possible. She persuaded Sire Records dance record promoter, Bobby Shaw, to let her accompany him on his visits to radio stations and dance clubs, where he would try to get Madonna's music played.

Madonna also attended promotional business meetings between Shaw and local Los Angeles DJs. She was serious at these meetings and paid close attention, taking copious notes. In the meetings, she learned many things about the music business, including how people made decisions about what songs got played on the radio and therefore had a chance of becoming successful.

Video Star

While Sire Records was promoting her music, Madonna contacted friends in the business to set up performances for her around the city. The most important of these was at Danceteria.

The performance allowed Madonna to demonstrate her visual appeal and dance abilities as well as showcase her music. Madonna worked for weeks organizing the details of her appearance, which would include a dance performance of "Everybody." She hired backup dancers and choreographed a complex performance.

Already a savvy businessperson, she knew that the Danceteria performance would be important for her career, so she invited

Madonna Means Business

From the beginning of her career, Madonna insisted on being in control as much as possible. Even after becoming famous, she discovered that, being a woman, she had to continue to prove herself to her producers so that they would take her seriously. Quoted in J. Randy Taraborrelli's book, *Madonna: An Intimate Biography*, Madonna says she had to overcome the sexist preconceptions of her Warner Brothers producers.

> Warner Bros. Records is a hierarchy of old men, and it's a chauvinist environment to be working in because I'm treated like this sexy little girl. . . . I have to prove them wrong, which has meant not only proving myself to my fans but to my record company as well. This is something that happens when you're a girl.
> It wouldn't happen to Prince or Michael Jackson. I had to do everything on my own and it was hard trying to convince people that I was worth a record deal. After that, I had the same problem trying to convince the record company that I had more to offer than a one-shot girl singer.

Throughout her career, Madonna has struggled to be taken seriously as a female artist in a male-dominated industry.

Madonna's video for "Everybody" was a hit on MTV and in dance clubs.

several Sire Records producers to the show. After seeing her perform, the producers were so impressed by her visual appeal that they decided to market Madonna's music on video. At the time, music videos were a new phenomenon. In August 1981, the cable network Music Television (MTV) had appeared on the air for the first time. It soon became popular, and within three years, bands began filming videos for MTV to help promote the sale of their albums.

The Sire Records producers thought MTV was a perfect showcase for Madonna, so they agreed to produce a low-budget video of her performing "Everybody." Sire Records distributed the video to MTV and to dance clubs, and the video became popular on TV and in the clubs. Madonna's career as a video star had begun.

"I Want to Rule the World!"

Madonna's second single, released in March 1983, featured the songs "Burning Up" and "Physical Attraction." She set out on an East Coast tour to promote the record, performing in nightclubs and giving radio and newspaper interviews. Sire Records executives agreed to produce a video for "Burning Up," spending thousands more dollars on the production than they had for her first video because "Everybody" had been so successful. Sire Records also agreed to produce Madonna's first full-length album, entitled *Madonna*.

Released in July 1983, the album was immediately successful. The song "Holiday" became the number one dance song in America, and in October 1983 entered *Billboard*'s Hot 100 pop singles chart. Several other singles from the album also became hits.

Thanks to this album, Madonna's popularity grew. Her music was played on major stations all over the United States, and her videos from the album appeared on MTV, launching a fashion craze as young girls imitated Madonna's clothing style. Biographer Barbara Victor writes: "Madonna inspired a national craze among teenagers and eventually among young adults with her lacy underwear, rosary beads as jewelry, Boy Toy belt buckles, and tousled blond hair with black roots."[33]

As Madonna became more popular and successful, she could no longer keep up with the business side of her career by herself. Thus, she hired Freddy DeMann, one of the most sought-after music agents in Hollywood. DeMann had represented many famous clients, including Michael Jackson. Madonna's relationship with DeMann lasted fifteen years and was one of the most successful partnerships in music history.

In January 1984, soon after being hired, DeMann arranged for Madonna to perform on the popular, long-running dance program *American Bandstand*, hosted by Dick Clark. The show was Madonna's first public television appearance. When Clark asked her what she wanted from her career, Madonna told Clark and the millions of television viewers, "I want to rule the world!"[34]

New Acting Career

Madonna was not exaggerating much when she made her announcement on *American Bandstand*. Not only did she want to become world famous as a musician, she also wanted to be a movie star. Ever since childhood, she had dreamed of being an actress. She thought that her rising fame in the music industry would help her begin a career in acting. Thus, in September 1983, DeMann arranged a meeting for her with Hollywood film producer Jon Peters. Peters cast Madonna in a very small role in his film *Vision Quest* (released in 1985). She spent November 1983 in Spokane, Washington, filming her part, but it was not exciting for her. She was bored by the shoot and disappointed with the brevity of her role.

Her music career continued to thrive, however, and this increased her chances of landing larger roles. In the summer of 1984, Madonna auditioned for a role in a comedy called *Desperately Seeking Susan*. In the film, a suburban housewife (played by

Trials of Fame

Shortly after the release of her debut album, Madonna experienced fame for the first time. Three years later, she was known worldwide. In a 1985 interview with journalist Denise Worrell for the *Time* magazine article entitled "Now: Madonna on Madonna," Madonna discussed the pros and cons of fame:

> I love being onstage and I love reaching out to people and I love the expressions in people's eyes and just the ecstasy and the thrill. But I have to have a bodyguard around me for security reasons. When I finish a show, I can't stop on the street and sign a few autographs because I would be there three years. Sometimes when I go back to my hotel room there are people hiding in the ice closet waiting. That is scary. . . . I feel caged in hotel rooms wherever I go. . . . The people don't want to hurt me. They just want to be near me. Actually, it hasn't gotten to the point where I never go out. I still go running on the street and shopping. I don't send people out to do everything for me. I want to try to do as many things as I can in that regard, because I think if you really separate yourself from people, you start to have a scary opinion of the world. I don't want to feel that way. I don't want to sit around and contemplate my fame and how popular I am.

Rosanna Arquette) becomes friends with a kooky, streetwise girl named Susan, the part for which Madonna auditioned. Producer Susan Seidelman felt Madonna was perfect for the role and hired the singer right away. It was a victory for Madonna's new acting career because she beat out several well-established actresses for

Madonna in a still from Desperately Seeking Susan. *Madonna won the lead role in that film in 1984.*

Madonna poses at the 1984 MTV Video Music Awards where she was honored for two videos from her debut album.

the role, including Kelly McGillis, Ellen Barkin, and Melanie Griffith.

Desperately Seeking Susan

Filming for *Desperately Seeking Susan* began in November 1984, the same time Madonna's latest single from her debut album,

Borderline, earned a place on *Billboard* magazine's Top Ten pop chart. Soon afterward, Madonna won two MTV Video Music Awards for videos from her debut album. Madonna used her increasing success to persuade Seidelman to make changes to the character of Susan. For instance, Madonna hated Susan's clothes and substituted her own. Further, the film was restructured so that Madonna could perform her new song "Into the Groove."

Several people who knew Madonna well said that the character of Susan ended up being extremely close to Madonna's personality. Kamins says, "[Susan] wasn't a character, it was Madonna. A wisecracking, smart-ass, gum-chewing, savvy, streetwise chick."[35] Even Madonna acknowledged the similarities between herself and the character, saying, "I shared a lot with Susan. She's a free spirit and does what she wants."[36]

With all the changes, the part of Susan became a primary character in the film. This annoyed Arquette, who had originally been cast as the only lead. Arquette tried unsuccessfully to leave the film in protest. Arquette says:

> It was completely unfair. As soon as Madonna came into the picture, the script was changed to suit her. I told [the producers] that if [the film] was going to be nothing more than a two-hour rock video spotlighting Madonna, well, I didn't want to be a part of it.[37]

But Arquette was unable to get out of her contract and stayed to make the film. Whatever negative feelings Arquette had about the film, by the time the movie was done, she and Madonna had become good friends.

The film was released in March 1985, only a month after *Vision Quest,* which had been delayed in postproduction for months. Although Madonna's performance in *Vision Quest* did not derive much notice (other than the fact that it helped sales of the soundtrack), her role in *Desperately Seeking Susan* won praise from many critics who loved Susan's charisma and strength. Film critic Judith Crist said that Madonna's Susan was "dripping self-confident savvy from every pore."[38] The film grossed $27.3 million in the United States, making it the fifth top-earning film

of 1985. Madonna was elated. After spending her youth yearn-
ing to appear on the movie screen, she had accomplished her
goal and begun her acting career.

Like a Virgin

On November 12, 1984, while Madonna was filming *Desperately
Seeking Susan*, her second album, *Like a Virgin*, was released.
Madonna wanted to use this album to develop her public image.
The image she chose and portrayed in the songs and videos was

Madonna used both her performance in Desperately Seeking Susan
and her second album, Like a Virgin, *to develop a streetwise, sexy, and
sassy public image.*

much like the character of Susan in *Desperately Seeking Susan*: street-smart, sexy, and wisecracking. Madonna also wanted to use the videos as tributes to the classic female movie stars she had so admired when she was young, especially Marilyn Monroe.

The videos shot to accompany *Like a Virgin* were high budget and lavish. They also emphasized Madonna's sex appeal and her identification with classic film stars. For instance, the video for her song "Material Girl" was a tribute to Marilyn Monroe and imitated Monroe's performance of the song "Diamonds Are a Girl's Best Friend," from the film *Gentlemen Prefer Blondes*. In the video, Madonna flirts with several tuxedo-clad dancers who lavish expensive gifts upon her.

Response to *Like a Virgin*

Like a Virgin was very successful. The title track, "Like a Virgin," became Madonna's first number one pop single and stayed at number one for six weeks. Other songs also did well. "Material Girl" rose to number two, and "Dress You Up" went to number five. The album also became a number one album on *Billboard* magazine's charts and was one of the best-selling records of 1985.

Although the sales of the album were high, the reviews were less enthusiastic. Many critics thought Madonna was not worth serious consideration because she seemed flighty, and the songs' lyrics were not sophisticated. Even other musicians spoke against her, including Rolling Stones front man Mick Jagger, who said that Madonna's songs were characterized by a "central dumbness."[39]

The videos for the album's title track, "Like a Virgin," also received negative criticism. Some feminists said the video perpetuated negative stereotypes about women. Filmed in Venice, Italy, part of the video featured Madonna, dressed in a white lingerie wedding dress, being swept off her feet by a man in a lion's mask. The feminist critics said that the images promoted the idea that women were passive and weak. Other critics said that the video's lyrics and content were too sexually explicit for television.

Madonna was surprised, however, saying that critics had misunderstood her intent with the song. She explains:

Madonna performs "Like a Virgin." The video for the hit title track generated controversy.

When I did the song, to me, I was singing about how something made me feel a certain way—brand-new and fresh—and everybody else interpreted it as, "I don't want to be a virgin anymore,". . . [but] that's not what I sang at all. . . . People have this idea that if you're sexual and beautiful and provocative, then there's nothing else you could possibly offer. . . . You *can* be sexy and strong at the same time.[40]

Sean Penn

Despite the negative reviews, 1985 was off to a good start for Madonna. In addition to her two film appearances, six singles from *Like a Virgin* were hits, and she had five video releases. She also met the man who would become her first husband.

In February 1985, while filming the video for "Material Girl" at Warner Brothers Studios in Hollywood, California, Madonna was approached by a young actor and fan named Sean Penn. Son of actress Eileen Ryan and director Leo Penn, Sean was a well-established young actor when he came to the soundstage to meet Madonna. The "Material Girl" video director, James Foley, was a friend of Penn's, and Foley asked Madonna if she would meet the young actor. She agreed, but recalls that she was aloof when the pair first met because she was distracted by work. She said hello and then rushed back to filming, leaving him standing in the wings of the soundstage. But Penn waited around until the end of the day so that he could speak to her again. Madonna liked his persistence and went to talk to him. She recalls:

> There were people everywhere, so it was hard for us to have this conversation but we were just kind of throwing questions at each other and being really provocative. Finally, when he was about to leave, I said, "Wait a minute, I have something for you." I had given flowers to everybody in the cast and the crew of the video . . . and I had one left so I ran back upstairs, and when I came back, I handed him a rose.[41]

Madonna liked Penn, but because she was dating the musician Prince at the time, she did not pursue her interest in him. A few weeks later, when the relationship with Prince ended, however, she telephoned Penn to arrange to see him again.

In Love

On their first date, Penn picked up Madonna in his car and drove them around Los Angeles. He showed her many tourist sights, including Marilyn Monroe's grave at Westwood Cemetery near

Hollywood. Then, Penn took her to a party at the home of his friend, filmmaker and actor Warren Beatty. Madonna, who had always wanted to be famous, was excited as Penn introduced her to the celebrities at the party, including Beatty, Jack Nicholson, and Mickey Rourke. She also met comic Sandra Bernhard, with whom she would later become close friends.

Upon returning to New York, Madonna told her friends about Penn. Several of them expressed concern. They were worried that Penn, a heavy drinker who had a reputation of being jealous and having a bad temper, was not a good match for her. Madonna, however, acknowledged and even liked Penn's reputation, saying that they were a lot alike. She said, "He's wild. . . . He'll probably die young some day. [But] we have so much in common . . . and have such similar temperaments. I feel like he's my brother or something."[42]

Madonna and Sean Penn at the Los Angeles premiere of At Close Range. *The pair met in 1985 on the set of the "Material Girl" video.*

Meanwhile, the press speculated that Madonna, still a novice actress, was dating Penn to use his Hollywood connections to advance her film career. Madonna ignored these rumors, and Madonna's friends insisted that she loved Penn, not his Hollywood status.

Engagement

During their courtship, Madonna and Penn spent much of their time on opposite ends of the country. Penn remained in Los Angeles, where he was busy with his film career, and Madonna was in New York preparing for a two-month nationwide tour to promote *Like a Virgin*. She was still a disciplined performer willing to put her personal life second to her career.

Arranged by Warner Brothers, the *Like a Virgin* tour began in April 1985 and quickly broke ticket-sale records in many cities. In New York City, for example, the show sold out in only twenty-four minutes.

During the tour, Penn met Madonna everywhere he could so they could spend time together. Then, in June 1985, the pair reunited in Tennessee, where Penn was working on his latest film, *At Close Range*. They spent two weeks together. At the end of their visit, Penn proposed marriage. Madonna accepted.

Publicity

Madonna and Penn's courtship and engagement was important news for the entertainment tabloid newspapers and magazines. And soon, the couple discovered that they had very different attitudes toward the press.

Madonna was, for the most part, eager to be in the spotlight and to have people interested in what she was doing. And the press accommodated her. In May 1985, she appeared on the cover of *Time* with the headline "Madonna: Why She's Hot." There were a few times, however, when she struggled with the publicity of her newfound stardom. Tabloid newspapers sometimes printed rumors or lies about her personal life, and in August 1985, *Playboy* and *Penthouse* magazines printed nude photographs of Madonna taken when she worked as a model in

Sean Penn in a movie still. Penn proposed marriage to Madonna after dating her for only a few months.

New York to make money. She confided to friends that, even though the photos did nothing to damage her popularity, she was upset about their publication because she had not been the one to release them. She says:

> The thing that annoyed me most wasn't so much that they were nude photographs but that I felt really out of control—for the first time in what I thought to be several years of careful planning and knowing what was going to happen. It took me by surprise.[43]

In contrast, Sean Penn did not like publicity at all. He had been a celebrity since he was an adolescent and tried to avoid press attention as much as possible. But, after his engagement to Madonna, aggressive photographers (often called paparazzi) followed the couple wherever they went, trying to catch them in private moments. Additionally, newspapers speculated that Madonna was already pregnant by Penn. Penn was angered by the rumors and the constant intrusion into their lives, and his public reaction was often violent.

On June 30, 1985, just a few weeks after their engagement, Penn was charged with assaulting two photographers outside his and Madonna's hotel room. Madonna was upset by the incident, but understood his frustration and anger toward the press. She says, "I've been dealing with the media since the very beginning of my career, and Sean never really had to. I wanted [the attention], and I was sort of ready to deal with it, and he wasn't."[44] Penn was given a one-thousand-dollar fine and a suspended jail term for the assault after pleading guilty to the charges.

Wedding in Malibu

While Madonna and Penn's courtship and engagement attracted the attention of the press, their wedding became a media event. The ceremony took place on August 16, 1985, Madonna's twenty-seventh birthday. Because the couple was concerned that the press would ruin their wedding, they did not give out any details about the ceremony or reception in the wedding invitations. Guests had to call a number listed on the invitation to find out where to show up. Even the caterers were not told where to go until the last minute.

The wedding was held in Malibu, California, at the home of Penn's friend Kurt Unger. The guest list included Madonna's and Penn's families as well as many celebrities, including Tom Cruise, Christopher Walken, Andy Warhol, Martin Sheen, Rosanna Arquette, Emilio Estevez, Timothy Hutton, Diane Keaton, and Judd Nelson. Also in attendance were Cher and talk-show host David Letterman.

Despite the precautions, the wedding's location was discovered by the press. Press helicopters carrying photographers hov-

Penn and Madonna married in August 1985. Despite precautions to ensure privacy, the event was a huge media circus.

ered overhead, and one hundred reporters and photographers waited outside the house's main gates, hoping to see the bride and groom leave. During the ceremony, the helicopters pulled in so close that the wind from the rotors blew the decorations and made it difficult for the guests to hear the couple exchange vows.

But the day was not all bad. Madonna recalls that although she was at first overwhelmed by the event, she was able to see the humor in it. "I didn't think I was going to be getting married with thirteen helicopters flying over my head. It turned into a circus. . . . At first I was outraged, and then I was laughing."[45]

After the wedding, the couple moved into a secluded Malibu estate. When asked by a reporter whether the house would have a fence to keep out the press, Penn jokingly replied, "A fence, nothing. We're going to have gun towers."[46]

Madonna's life underwent many changes during the early 1980s. When she first arrived in New York, she had been a struggling dancer. By her 1985 wedding, she was one of the richest and most popular performers in the country. Despite this accomplishment, Madonna believed that her greatest triumphs still lay ahead of her, and she was right. But there would be many troubles ahead as well.

Chapter 4

Troubles and Triumphs

T HE LATE 1980s were difficult for Madonna. She continued to drive her career forward, but, while her music career was never better, her acting career faltered. Additionally, her 1985 marriage to Penn became troubled soon after their wedding and deteriorated to divorce by the end of 1988.

Shanghai Surprise

As Madonna and Penn began their marriage, Madonna's ambition to further her acting career continued to be important to her. She wanted the variety that acting provided. "Music was still very important to me," she says, "but I always had a great interest in films, and the thought that I could only make records for the rest of my life filled me with horror."[47]

To help her with her acting career and to enable them to work together, Penn arranged for Madonna to appear with him in his next film, *Shanghai Surprise*. Set in 1930s China, the film was a comedy about a Christian missionary named Gloria Tatlock (played by Madonna) who becomes involved with a gangster (played by Penn). Filming began in China in January 1986, and difficulties quickly arose between the film's director, Jim Goddard, and the Penns. Madonna and Penn both thought the director did not know what he was doing and argued with him constantly.

For his part, Goddard cited Madonna's acting inexperience as a problem. In *Desperately Seeking Susan*, Madonna played a character whose personality was very close to her own, but for

Shanghai Surprise she had been cast against type, meaning the character was very different from her own personality; Gloria Tatlock was a quiet, well-mannered, and passive woman. Goddard complained that Madonna was too inexperienced as an actress to play the character and was frustrated because he

AIDS Activist

During her life, Madonna developed close friendships with several gay men. Many of these friends, including her dance teacher Christopher Flynn and artists Martin Burgoyne and Keith Haring, contracted acquired immune deficiency syndrome (AIDS) and died from the disease. Early in her career, Madonna decided to become an AIDS activist to honor these friends and help fight the disease, as biographer Andrew Morton describes in his book, *Madonna*:

> In response to [her friends'] deaths, she has quietly donated considerable sums to AIDS research and to the care of those suffering from the virus. She is also a champion of safe sex and gay rights, as well as a staunch advocate of the promotion of greater public awareness about the disease. To this end she has attended numerous charity events, freely lending her name and support to AIDS-related causes. In 1991 she became the first recipient of the AmFAR (American Foundation for AIDS Research) Award for Courage for her charitable work and AIDS-awareness efforts, while even conservative estimates put the money she has raised for AIDS charities at over $5 million.

Madonna speaks about raising AIDS awareness in 1998.

said she did not recognize when her performance was poor. According to Goddard:

> She didn't have a clue what she was doing. She was only good in the love scenes with Sean [Penn] because she really loved the guy. . . . In the rest [of the scenes] she was very wooden because she was so inexperienced. She would just walk through a scene and think she had given a fine performance when it was nothing of the sort.[48]

Sean Penn and Madonna in Shanghai Surprise. *Penn arranged to have Madonna star alongside him in the MGM comedy.*

Poison Penns

The production of *Shanghai Surprise* was also made difficult by problems between the Penns and the press. For instance, while filming in Macao, China, Leonel Borralho, a newspaper publisher and photographer, sued Penn for 1 million dollars after Penn and his bodyguard allegedly assaulted Borralho; the photographer had surprised Penn and Madonna as they entered their hotel, jumping out from behind a service door. Then, while in London during a few weeks of shooting on location, Madonna's driver ran her car over a photographer's foot when the man ran alongside the vehicle, trying to take a photograph of her. The press retaliated for these and other incidents by dubbing Madonna and Penn the "Poison Penns."

When the film was complete, Madonna and Penn returned to the United States and embarked on a publicity tour, appearing on several talk shows to promote the film. During the tour, they spoke about their difficulties with Goddard and discouraged viewers from seeing the movie.

Domestic Troubles

The professional difficulties with *Shanghai Surprise* were compounded by personal difficulties in Madonna and Penn's marriage. Years later, Penn admitted that he was an alcoholic during his marriage to Madonna. Further, he was frequently jealous and often had a violent temper. The tensions in the couple's marriage came to a head in April 1986 at a Los Angeles nightclub when Penn assaulted songwriter Dan Wolinski, an old friend of Madonna's. Wolinski kissed Madonna on the cheek in greeting, and Penn lost his temper; he beat up Wolinski and hit him with a chair. Penn was fined one thousand dollars and given a one-year probation, but Madonna was upset and embarrassed. A friend of Madonna's explains: "This was the first major stress, the first really traumatic episode for her. Wolinski was someone she knew, and it really shook her up."[49]

Penn was charged with assault again in August for beating up a photographer outside the couple's New York apartment. Again, he was fined and given probation.

Madonna in a movie still. Madonna began to see her husband's dark side during production of Shanghai Surprise.

These incidents and many others created negative publicity for both Penn and Madonna. Although Madonna refused to speak to the press about the troubles, friends said that she was frustrated that Penn's actions were making publicity a problem for the first time in her life. She told a friend, "Do you remember the time when I would do anything to get noticed? Now I spend all day hiding."[50]

Controversy

Madonna's personal life was not the only focus of public scrutiny. Her third album, *True Blue*, also garnered a lot of publicity when it was released in June 1986. Madonna coproduced the album and wrote the lyrics to all but one of the songs; she had written very few songs for her other albums. Several songs from *True Blue* were hits, but one single, "Papa Don't Preach," got a great deal of attention.

Madonna hugs Danny Aiello in the "Papa Don't Preach" video. The song, about an unwed pregnant woman who decides to keep her baby, caused quite a stir.

The song is about an unmarried girl who becomes pregnant and tells her father that she wants to keep her baby. When it was released, "Papa Don't Preach" received strong reactions from both sides of the teen pregnancy debate. The National Organization for Women (NOW), which encourages birth control and supports abortion rights, criticized Madonna for condoning teenage pregnancy. On the other hand, some religious groups praised the song as being antiabortion. Debates about the song's message appeared in newspaper and magazine editorials and articles.

In response, Madonna said she had no political intention with the song, but knew when she recorded it that it would be misinterpreted. She explains: "'Papa Don't Preach' is a message song that everyone is going to take the wrong way. Immediately they're going to say I am advising every young girl to go out and get pregnant."[51] Rather than encouraging teen pregnancy, she says that her intent with the song had been only to portray a teenage girl who was faced with a serious dilemma.

More Bad Publicity

After the release of *True Blue*, Penn and Madonna wanted to work together again. Penn had been cast as a gangster in the play *Goose and Tom-Tom* at the Lincoln Center Theater workshop in New York. He arranged for Madonna to play the only female part in the play, that of a gun moll, a gangster's girlfriend. The performance was not open to the public. Instead it was reserved for an invitation-only audience of friends of the cast. Actors and artists, including Warren Beatty, Tom Cruise, Melanie Griffith, and Andy Warhol made up the audience.

Again there were problems with the press. Following the August 29 performance, Penn and Madonna left Lincoln Center, where the play was performed, went to dinner, and then walked home to their apartment. There, a few photographers waited. When the photographers followed the couple, Madonna began shouting at them to stop taking pictures. Then Penn got into a fight with two of the photographers. The rest of the photographers took pictures of the fight and the next day the incident appeared in magazines and newspapers all over the world.

Madonna stars as Nikki Finn in the romantic comedy Who's That Girl?

At the same time, *Shanghai Surprise* was released by MGM/United Artists. Critics panned the film, accusing both Penn and Madonna of poor performances. Public response to the film was also terrible, and it earned less than $2.3 million total.

Who's That Girl?

Although Penn and Madonna expected the negative response to *Shanghai Surprise*, Madonna was concerned that the film's failure, combined with the bad press the couple was receiving, would have a negative impact on her career. So she wanted to do another film soon to put the bad press behind her.

After the run of *Goose and Tom-Tom*, Penn left for Los Angeles to begin work on a new film, and Madonna stayed in New York to audition for the lead role in a movie called *Who's That Girl?* The film was a comedy about a wrongly accused female ex-convict named Nikki Finn. Finn kidnaps a lawyer to help her find out who really committed the crimes for which she was imprisoned. Madonna's friend James Foley, who hoped to direct the film, gave her the script. On his recommendation, she read it, and she liked the Finn character.

The movie's producers, however, were concerned. Penn's recent legal troubles made them hesitant to hire Madonna because they feared bad publicity. But in the end, they hired her anyway. They also gave Foley the director's job, a choice that pleased Madonna. Foley had directed several of her music videos and had been the best man at her wedding to Penn. After her negative experience with *Shanghai Surprise*, Madonna looked forward to working with a director she trusted and liked.

On the Set Again

Madonna enjoyed filming *Who's That Girl?*, but her acting inexperience showed again. She was unable to tell when she was not acting well and thus did not want to reshoot scenes when Foley asked her to. Nonetheless, Madonna was always punctual and serious about the work. She also became the film's musical director and spent her evenings in the studio recording songs for the movie's soundtrack.

Who's That Girl? was released in August 1987 and was a critical and box-office failure. The film cost $20 million to make but earned only $2.55 million. Further, the reviews were poor for the movie in general and for Madonna's performance in particular.

The poor response to *Who's That Girl?* did not detract from the success of the film's soundtrack, however. The songs Madonna wrote for the album became hits, and album sales were so good that Warner Brothers decided to send Madonna on her first world tour—the *Who's That Girl?* tour—in the fall of 1987.

More Domestic Troubles

The following spring, Sean Penn's legal problems and alcoholism put more strain on his and Madonna's marriage. In

April, Penn was charged with assaulting an actor while on the set of his new film, *Colors;* a month later, he was arrested for drunk driving. The drunk driving incident violated the conditions of his probation for a 1985 assault conviction, and he was sent to jail for sixty days. As a result, he was unable to attend Madonna's *Who's That Girl?* tour.

Madonna told the press that the experience would help Penn. "I think Sean will emerge from jail as a better person and an even greater actor."[52] Despite this show of support, after his release from jail, Penn acknowledged that his trouble with the law was affecting his relationship with Madonna. "Going to jail is not good for any marriage,"[53] he said.

Trouble with the Press

Madonna's first husband, Sean Penn, was arrested numerous times during their marriage for assaulting photographers and reporters. In a September 10, 1987, interview for *Rolling Stone* reporter Mikal Gilmore's article, "The Madonna Mystique," Madonna discussed Penn's antagonistic relationship with the press and how it differed from her own:

> [Sean] will always deal with the press in his own way. For myself, I have accommodated the press a great deal. . . . [These incidents with the press] have been traumatic. I mean, I don't like violence. I never condone hitting anyone, and I never thought that any violence should have taken place. But on the other hand, I understood Sean's anger, and believe me, I've wanted to hit them many times. I never *would*, you know, because I realize that it would make things worse. Besides, I have chances to vent my anger in other ways than confrontation. I like to fight people and kind of manipulate them into feeling like they're not being fought . . . I'd rather do it that way. But yes, those were very traumatic experiences for me . . . I think Sean really believes that [the incidents] are a waste of energy. It antagonizes the press more and generates more publicity. . . . But once they realized he was a target, they really went out of their way to pick on him, to the point where they would walk down the street and kind of poke on him, say, "C'mon, c'mon, hit me, hit me." It's not fair. And they insult me, and they try to get him to react that way, so, God, you just have to have the strength to rise above it.

Due to this strain, Madonna and Penn separated in November 1987, and Madonna filed for divorce on December 4. A friend of Madonna's says that the singer was reluctant to resort to divorce, however. "She was completely distraught," says her friend. "'I don't want a divorce,' she told me, 'but I don't know what else to do.'"[54]

Despite this realization, later in December Madonna withdrew the divorce papers without explanation. The marriage was still in trouble, however. That Christmas, while living in New York, Madonna met John F. Kennedy Jr., the son of the late U.S. president, John F. Kennedy. They began dating, and the affair lasted for several months in early 1988 while Penn lived at his and Madonna's Malibu home.

Speed-the-Plow

While dating Kennedy and living in New York, Madonna, not discouraged by the bad reviews of *Who's That Girl?*, pursued more acting roles. In December 1987, she auditioned for the role of Karen in writer David Mamet's play, *Speed-the-Plow*, a three-character comedy about life in Hollywood. Director Gregory Mosher was doubtful about casting Madonna. He worried that her notoriety would detract from the play. "You don't want a play that you have worked on for five years to be overshadowed by a rock star,"[55] he explains. But Madonna did well in her audition, and Mosher cast her. The play opened on Broadway in 1988.

Reviews were favorable for the play, but mixed for Madonna's performance. Although one reviewer acknowledged Madonna's charm and another praised her for "scrupulously disciplined comic acting," the New York *Daily News* review represented the majority of the response to Madonna's acting, claiming: "NO SHE CAN'T ACT." Dennis Cunningham, theater critic for CBS-TV, said, "Her ineptitude is scandalously thorough."[56]

Madonna, now used to criticism about her acting, thought that negative reviews for her work were inevitable. She said, "[Critics] always say horrible things about me. They'll be saying those things the rest of my life."[57]

Madonna plays the role of Karen in David Mamet's play Speed-the-Plow.

Despite the mixed reviews, Madonna's appearance in the play helped box-office sales. *Speed-the-Plow* sold a record number of advance tickets and made more than $1 million.

A New Role

Soon after she finished performing in *Speed-the-Plow*, Madonna became interested in *Dick Tracy*, a new film produced and directed by Warren Beatty. Based on a popular 1930s comic strip, *Dick Tracy* would star an ensemble cast of well-known actors, including Al Pacino, Dustin Hoffman, and Beatty himself as Dick Tracy.

Madonna wanted to play the role of Breathless Mahoney, a femme fatale and the lead female part in the film. Beatty was not confident in her acting ability, however, so he met Madonna for dinner to discuss it. At the end of the evening, Beatty agreed to hire her. But Madonna would have to work for Screen Actor's Guild scale wages of $1,440 a week, much less money than she was used to earning. Certain that *Dick Tracy* was going to be a success, Madonna agreed, believing that an appearance in the film would help her acting career. Her contract also provided her with a percentage of the box-office sales and merchandising rights for the film, as well as a large percentage of the profits for the soundtrack, which would include a number of songs performed by her.

Divorce

Just before the production of *Dick Tracy* began, Madonna returned to live in Malibu. Because of their continuing marital difficulties, Penn went to live with his father. Soon after, Madonna began dating Warren Beatty. Penn found out about the affair and

Madonna as Breathless Mahoney in Dick Tracy. *Madonna also signed on to do the soundtrack for the film.*

Penn and Madonna react to the press. Their marriage was marred by difficulties from the start, and in January 1989 the couple divorced.

became jealous. On December 28, 1988, Penn went to the Malibu house and the couple had a fight. By then, both of them knew their marriage was over. Madonna filed for divorce again, and the marriage was officially dissolved on January 25, 1989.

Madonna blamed the failure of her first marriage in part on the public nature of the couple's life. She explains:

I felt that no one wanted us to be together. They celebrated our union, and then they wanted us to be apart. There were rumors about us getting a divorce a week after the wedding. We fought that. And, yes, that is difficult. I don't know if anyone can do it [under those circumstances]. You have to be really, really strong and immune. Very sure of yourself.[58]

Certainly her private life had been the source of media speculation, particularly since her marriage to Penn. But as the 1980s came to a close, her professional career got a lot of attention as well. And in 1989, she entered the most tumultuous and controversial period of her life.

Chapter 5

Controversy

DURING THE SIX years following her divorce from Sean Penn, Madonna experienced increasing popularity and recognition as a musician, performer, and businessperson. These years were also the most controversial of her life to date. As she sought to shock audiences and critics, many critics and fans reacted negatively to her career choices.

"Like a Prayer"

A month after filing for divorce from Penn, Madonna signed a $5-million contract with the Pepsi-Cola company to do a commercial based on her yet-to-be-released video for the song "Like a Prayer." As part of the agreement, Pepsi also agreed to provide another $5 million in funding for Madonna's upcoming 1990 *Blonde Ambition* World Tour.

Released in March 1989, "Like a Prayer" was the title track on her upcoming album by the same name. Dedicated to her mother, "who taught me to pray,"[59] the record contained several dance-pop songs and some serious ones, including "Like a Prayer" and "Till Death Do Us Part," which Madonna said was inspired in part by her marriage to Penn. Madonna cowrote ten songs on the album and wrote none by herself. The lyrics reflected personal changes she had experienced. She says, "I wanted the album to speak to things on my mind. It was a complex time in my life."[60]

The Pepsi commercial based on "Like a Prayer" was entitled "Make a Wish," and it was first televised on March 2, 1989. In the United States it appeared during the highest-rated show on television at the time, *The Cosby Show*. The commercial was a wholesome video showing Madonna dancing and singing with an eight-year-old girl to the gospel sounds of the song "Like a Prayer." Of the commercial, Madonna said, "It's very, very sweet. It's very sentimental."[61]

Controversy began, however, when the "Like a Prayer" video played on MTV for the first time on March 3, 1989, the day after the Pepsi commercial aired. Religious groups were upset by the sexual and religious imagery in the video. Biographer Mark Bego describes the video as emotional, religiously symbolic, and controversial:

> In Madonna's "Like a Prayer" video, she witnesses a murder, runs into a church wearing only a brown slip,

Madonna poses in the "Like a Prayer" video. The video's powerful religious and sexual imagery upset many religious groups.

kisses a statue of a saint, makes love with a black man on a church pew, dances in front of burning crosses, sings with a church choir, and shows bleeding stigmata on both palms as though she had survived a crucifixion. Only Madonna could pull this video off—it is stormy, mysterious, tragic, violent, dark, and exciting.[62]

Pepsi Pulls Out

Immediately after MTV aired the video, numerous religious groups condemned it as offensive, citing the visual references to the crucifixion of Christ as blasphemous. The video was even banned in Italy, where a Roman Catholic group protested.

Similar outrage took hold in the United States. Several religious groups threatened boycotts against Pepsi. In particular, Reverend Donald E. Wildmon of the American Family Association (AFA), a Christian group, threatened a one-year boycott of all Pepsi products by AFA's 380,000 members if the Pepsi Company did not dissolve its partnership with Madonna and discontinue airing the "Make a Wish" commercial. In an interview with *Time* magazine, Wildmon explained that his group targeted Pepsi because the company's support of Madonna's career linked it to her, making Pepsi in part responsible for her "Like a Prayer" video. Wildmon said:

> Pepsi said to our young people in this country, "Here is the role model we think worthy of $10 million in support. Here is a pop singer who makes a video that's sacrilegious to the core. Here's a pop star that made a low-budget porn film" . . . [Pepsi] can do that. They've got every right. . . . All I'm saying is "Don't ask me to buy Pepsi if you do it."[63]

Pepsi responded to the pressure by meeting Wildmon's demands. The company canceled the commercial and withdrew its promised funding for Madonna's tour. However, Madonna was able to keep the $5 million for the commercial. The controversy over the video actually increased the song's popularity and sales of the album. Within three weeks, *Like a Prayer* was the

Despite the controversy surrounding the "Like a Prayer" video, Madonna enjoyed considerable artistic and commercial success in 1989.

best-selling record in America, and it went on to top music charts all over the world. The "Like a Prayer" video also won the 1989 MTV's Viewer's Choice Award. In her acceptance speech for that award, Madonna acknowledged that the controversy had helped the video. "I'd like to thank Pepsi for causing so much controversy,"[64] she said.

Praise for Madonna

In addition to the Viewer's Choice honor, at the end of 1989 Madonna also received recognition for her business abilities. *Forbes* magazine recognized her as the second-largest money-maker for 1988 and 1989, second only to musician Bruce Springsteen. In addition to her performance earnings, Madonna also established three companies: Boy Toy Records, Slutco Video, and Siren Films. Madonna served as president for all three companies.

Madonna, however, downplayed her financial success. In an April 1990 interview, she said: "Part of the reason I'm successful is because I'm a good businesswoman, but I don't think it is necessary for people to know that. . . . The public shouldn't think about it."[65]

Even so, the *Forbes* honor was deserved. Between 1986 and 1990, she had earned approximately $100 million, making her one of the most powerful people in entertainment. And she was proud of her accomplishment. She says, "It's a great feeling to be powerful. I've been striving for it all my life. I think that's just the quest of every human being: power."[66]

Response to *Dick Tracy*

Although Madonna was recognized for her business sense, she continued to struggle with her acting career. Poor reviews for her

Fear of Mediocrity

Madonna has gained a reputation among those who work with her as a highly disciplined and ambitious person. But in an April 1991 interview with Lynn Hirschberg for a *Vanity Fair* article entitled "The Misfit," she revealed that much of her drive comes from a fear of mediocrity.

> All of my will has always been to conquer some horrible feeling of inadequacy. I'm always struggling with that fear. . . . Again and again. My drive in life is from this horrible fear of being mediocre. And that's always pushing me, pushing me. Because even though I've become Somebody, I still have to prove that I'm *Somebody*. My struggle has never ended and it probably never will.

films and theater projects continued to plague her. However, she achieved some success in June 1990, when *Dick Tracy* was released. Although critics were disappointed with the film in general, many liked Madonna's performance, particularly her singing on the soundtrack. Madonna performed the soundtrack's songs as Breathless Mahoney, and critic Mark Coleman praised her, saying she made the songs believable: "More than you'd expect, Madonna measures up to the challenging new material. . . . Even during this album's most melodramatic or self-conscious moments . . . Madonna never sounds as though she's 'just acting.'"[67]

Madonna as Breathless Mahoney. Although Dick Tracy *was poorly received, many critics praised Madonna's performance.*

Madonna performs a concert on her controversial Blonde Ambition *tour.*

On the business side, Madonna also made a lot of money from the film. Even though she worked for Screen Actor's Guild scale wages of $1,440 a week, she made almost $14 million from the soundtrack, and *Forbes* magazine estimated that she took home approximately $5 million from her percentage of box-office and merchandising revenues.

Blonde Ambition

While married to Sean Penn, Madonna had been resistant to talk about her personal life, but after her divorce she again enjoyed the media's attention. She said, "It's flattering to me that people take the time to analyze me and that I've so infiltrated their psyches. . . . I'd rather be on their minds than off."[68]

In March 1990, Madonna saw the opportunity to make use of the public attention toward her personal life. She hired a young Harvard film school graduate, Alex Kesheshian, to film a documentary of her upcoming *Blonde Ambition* tour. Beginning in May 1990, the tour would promote the release of her newest album, *I'm Breathless*, which featured three songs from the motion picture soundtrack of *Dick Tracy* as well as a new hit, "Vogue."

The *Blonde Ambition* tour was theatrical and elaborate. It featured lavish sets, designer costumes, and complex, choreographed dance numbers performed by Madonna and a troupe of young dancers. The tour was also extremely controversial because of the adult themes of the performances. For instance, Madonna appeared in various revealing or provocative costumes—one featured a cone-shaped breastplate—and mimicked sexual intercourse onstage with her male dancers.

Truth or Dare

From March—two months before the tour began—until it ended in September 1990, Kesheshian followed Madonna almost everywhere with a movie camera. When complete, the film was titled *Truth or Dare*, and in addition to concert footage it included personal scenes from Madonna's life. It featured, for instance, her first visit in many years to her mother's gravesite and contained scenes of Madonna in her role as boss and businessperson. She provided advice to her dancers, made business deals on the telephone in her hotel rooms, and responded to problems in performances.

The film also included material that some critics claimed was in bad taste. In one such scene, Madonna flashed her breasts to the camera. In another, she interviewed her male dancers in bed while they disrobed for the camera. She also lost her temper with dancers and crew, talked about her brother Martin's alcoholism, and reflected on her failed marriage with Penn.

Madonna was willing to answer her critics, however. When asked in an interview for *Rolling Stone* magazine if she thought the film was too personally revealing, Madonna explained that she decided to reveal as much of her personality as possible in the film, even if the depiction was unflattering at times. She said, "If I'm going to make a documentary and tell the director that I want to reveal truths, then I'm not going to say, 'But this is where I draw the line.' If you take all those parts out, what would you have?"[69]

Madonna in Truth or Dare. *The movie includes concert footage from the* Blonde Ambition *tour and personal scenes from Madonna's life.*

"Justify My Love"

Soon after her *Blonde Ambition* tour, Madonna got involved in a new controversy, this time over her video for the song "Justify My Love." In November 1990, Warner Brothers released *The Immaculate Collection*, Madonna's first greatest hits album. Also released was a companion video collection, which included Madonna's most popular videos from her entire career to date. The album and the video collection also included her newest effort, "Justify My Love."

Described by critic Brian D. Johnson as "a soft-core portrayal of an omni-sexual interlude at a hotel,"[70] "Justify My Love" was banned by MTV due to its adult themes and graphic sexuality. Angry, Madonna appeared in an interview on the news program *Nightline* to defend the video. During the broadcast, the video was shown for the first time on television.

Some in the media thought that Madonna made the video with the intention of creating controversy and using that controversy to her benefit, as had happened with her "Like a Prayer" video. Journalist Jay Cocks suggested as much in an article he wrote for *Time:* "Surely Madonna must have known she was provoking a showdown [with MTV], just as surely as she knew what to do when it happened."[71]

On *Nightline*, Madonna did admit that the publicity over the video would help sales. "In the end, you're going to wind up making even more money than you would have [if the video had been accepted by MTV]," said host Forrest Sawyer. Madonna replied, "Yeah. So lucky me."[72]

Whether or not Madonna had anticipated the outcome, the publicity surrounding the "Justify My Love"-MTV controversy did seem to help video sales. At the time of her *Nightline* appearance, retailers had placed and paid for more than 250,000 preorders for the yet-unseen video. And upon its release in December 1990, the video sold more than 400,000 copies.

Response and Controversy

Controversy and publicity, however, did not benefit *Truth or Dare* upon its release six months later. Critical response to the

Madonna appears at a screening of Truth or Dare *in an outfit as racy as any in the movie.*

documentary was mostly negative. Some reviewers said the film was Madonna's attempt to gain more publicity and attention. Stanley Kauffman of *The New Republic* calls the film "the exhibitionism of a . . . pure exhibitionist,"[73] and film critic Ralph Novak says the film was an exercise in self-promotion. Novak writes: "If in fact the film reveals anything about Madonna it is—surprise!— —that she is relentlessly engaged in trying to sell herself."[74]

Popular response to the film was better, but not as enthusiastic as Madonna had hoped, The film earned only $15 million at the box office. As the executive producer of the documentary, Madonna had invested $4 million in the film, so she did not lose money. But she had expected the film to be much more profitable.

Truth or Dare also caused controversy after its release. In 1992, three of the dancers who appeared in the film sued Madonna. They alleged that the footage shot of them while they were offstage invaded their privacy, and they complained that they were not paid for their appearance in the film. Madonna felt betrayed by the lawsuit. She had been friends with the dancers and felt she had compensated them for their appearances with numerous expensive gifts. The lawsuit persisted for two years, but never went to court. In 1994, Madonna settled the lawsuit and paid the dancers an undisclosed sum.

SEX

These controversies—*Truth or Dare* and "Justify My Love"—paled in comparison to the next one: Madonna's book, *Sex*, published in October 1992. *Sex* was a 128-page spiral-bound book with stainless steel covers. It was filled with erotic photographs of Madonna and accompanying text written by her. Madonna intended the book to be a provocative look at sexual identity and fantasy in a post-AIDS world. She even warned the public before the book's publication that it would shock many people. But she did not anticipate the level of controversy that arose.

A month before the book's release, the book's Japanese publisher, Haruki Kadokawa, initially refused to publish it in the Far East. He thought the photographs in it were too explicit. Only when Time Warner, the book's American publisher, threatened a lawsuit for breach of contract did he finally publish the book.

The response in America was not much better. Upon the book's publication, several booksellers in the southern United States were threatened with arrest on obscenity charges for selling *Sex* in their stores; charges were never filed. At the same time, libraries grappled with the problem of how to deal with the book. Some public librarians refused to order the book on the grounds that it did not meet their selection requirements. Many of those who did order the book faced protests by the community. Madonna, herself, received hate mail in response to the book.

She got up to two hundred letters a day from individuals and groups angered and offended by the book. Some of the letters even contained death threats. Even so, the book was a commercial success, going on to sell 1.5 million copies around the world.

Critical response to *Sex* was overwhelmingly negative, however. Most reviewers panned the book, and a professional literary committee, the Coogler Prize Committee, voted *Sex* the worst book of 1992.

The controversy and the negative response to *Sex* had a lasting effect on the next several years of Madonna's career. In a 1997 interview with *Rolling Stone*, Madonna said that the criticism changed the way the press treated her. She said, "People didn't attack me in a personal way before the book. After the book, they did. I'm talking about criticizing everything from my choice of men to my body—things that have nothing to do with my work."[75]

Erotica

The negative response to *Sex* was still just beginning when Madonna released her next album, *Erotica*, in November 1992, a month after the book's publication. Coproduced by Sire Records, Warner Brothers, and Madonna's own record company, Maverick, which she started in April of the same year, the album's liner notes contained photographs similar to those found in *Sex*. As a result, it became the only one of Madonna's albums to carry a parental advisory label. The videos from the album, particularly

Woman of Substance

During her career, Madonna was frequently criticized by the press as being superficial. But in a 1991 *Vanity Fair* article entitled "The Misfit," written by Lynn Hirschberg, Freddy DeMann, Madonna's agent for almost fifteen years, says that this perception is inaccurate.

What you have to understand with Madonna is that she has substance. People forget that. Since she reinvents herself all the time and does these provocative things, people tend to concentrate on her image of the moment. But there is substance there. If you only resort to provocation, you don't last long [in the music business].

the one from the title track, "Erotica," were also controversial because of their sexual imagery. In the video for "Erotica," for instance, Madonna appears as a masked dominatrix.

The album did not do as well as her previous albums had, but it was not a failure, going on to sell more than 3 million copies. Even so, Madonna later regretted releasing *Erotica* so soon after *Sex*. She felt the album was one of her strongest and that the book affected everything she did afterwards. "I love [*Erotica*], and it was overlooked," she says. "Everything I did for the next three years was dwarfed by my book."[76]

Failures

During the early 1990s, some writers, such as rock critic and biographer J. Randy Taraborrelli, suggested that Madonna had lost some of her fan support by being too controversial. Tarraborrelli wrote:

> Many of her fans, as well as critics, were asking if Madonna had gone too far. The release of the *Truth or Dare* film, the *Sex* book, and the *Erotica* album and video served to answer that question for some with a resounding "Yes!"[77]

Even Madonna herself was concerned by her recent critical failures. She worried how they would affect response to her future work.

Her next two films compounded her concern. Both released in 1993, *Body of Evidence* and *Dangerous Game* did very poorly. Despite what critics thought were strong performances on Madonna's part, the films were critical and box-office flops.

The Girlie Show

In October 1993, while audiences and critics panned her latest film efforts, Madonna embarked on her *Girlie Show* World Tour, a twenty-date, four-continent tour. The concert featured many songs from *Erotica* and some earlier material, and it sold out around the world.

Despite the strong negative response to *Sex*, Madonna's fourth tour included explicit content that led to more contro-

Madonna in a scene from the 1993 film Body of Evidence. *The movie did very poorly at the box office.*

versy. In Puerto Rico, there was outcry after her concert. Journalists claimed Madonna had desecrated the country's flag by rubbing it between her legs. And an Israel performance was canceled because of protests by Orthodox Jews who said the show was obscene.

Nonetheless, the concert was another financial success. It was also admired by most critics. Madonna was still a great performer and entertained audiences with a stunning and often funny show. After seeing her perform at Wembley Stadium in London, critic Thom Duffy said that Madonna's sense of humor was the surprise amidst the lavish production. He wrote:

[The show] offered enough titillation for the excitable British press, but the real "shock" was the humor and warmth Madonna brought to her production, with its big-top staging, Broadway choreography and nods to numerous pop icons of the past.[78]

With *The Girlie Show*, Madonna ended the year well. After suffering so much negative publicity in the last years, she enjoyed the critical and popular praise of her tour. Biographer Andrew Morton writes:

"The Girlie Show" enabled Madonna to end the difficult year 1993 on a successful note. Many observers and fans considered it to be her best show to date, reaffirming that, as a singer and stage performer—if not a movie star—Madonna could still please her audience. Still, she was now more sensitive than ever to criticism, probably because she'd had to endure so much of it in recent times. Even the slightest negative tone to a review would send her reeling.[79]

Embarrassment

Although she was sensitive to negative criticism, Madonna brought more bad publicity upon herself when she appeared on a talk show in early 1994. In March, a few months after returning from *The Girlie Show* Tour, Madonna appeared on *The Late Show with David Letterman* and gave an interview she later regretted.

In what one critic called a "last-ditch attempt to be shocking, sexy, and controversial,"[80] Madonna tried to annoy and embarrass host Letterman. She asked him personal questions about his sex life and then said so many obscene words that network censors had to cover up, or bleep out, most of her side of the conversation. She also made sexually explicit jokes and insulted Letterman but did not get laughs from the audience. When Letterman tried to cut the segment short, Madonna at first refused to leave the stage, even when members of the audience booed.

Even though the show received very high ratings, Madonna received a lot of criticism in the press for being childish and obscene. Of her appearance on *Late Show*, Matt Roush in *USA Today* said, "Madonna reclaimed her title as the raunchiest act on TV with a bizarre, combative and shock-a-minute appearance."[81]

Even Madonna's friend, actress and talk-show host Rosie O'Donnell, was shocked by Madonna's behavior and asked her why she had acted as she had. According to O'Donnell, Madonna said that *Late Show* producers had encouraged her to do it and that she was angry about the way it turned out. "She

Madonna performs dressed as the Indian deity Shiva during her Girlie Show *tour.*

In 1998, Madonna said she regretted her behavior during a March 1994 appearance on The Late Show with David Letterman.

was pretty [upset] about it," says O'Donnell. "She said she didn't really want to do it. She said she knew better at this point in her career than to do it, but that she listened to [the producers] . . . It was a mistake."[82]

A few years later, Madonna reflected on her appearance on *Late Show.* In a 1998 interview, she blamed her bad behavior on her anger at the press. She said:

> That was a time in my life when I was extremely angry.
> . . . The press was constantly beating up on me, and I felt like I was a victim. So I lashed out at people and [Letterman] was one of them. And I am not particularly proud of it.[83]

Time for a Change

The controversies and the negative publicity surrounding Madonna's career during the first few years of the 1990s changed her. Although she remained determined to provoke and challenge her audience and critics, she realized that she needed to reconnect with them as well. Additionally, as she looked toward the coming years, Madonna also thought about transforming her personal life; she wanted to have a family. Madonna had already changed her persona numerous times during her career. But as she approached the new millennium, she was to undertake her most drastic transformation yet.

Chapter 6

Reinvention and Self-Discovery

MADONNA WAS ONE of the richest women in the music industry by the mid-1990s. Her *Girlie Show* tour had sold out all over the world, her albums made millions of dollars each year, and her record label Maverick produced one of the best-selling albums of 1995, Alanis Morrisette's *Jagged Little Pill*.

While her book, her music, and her documentary made a great deal of money, Madonna felt that her career and personal life choices in the early 1990s had hurt her public image. She was concerned that critics and audiences focused more on the negative publicity and the controversies surrounding her book, music, and videos than her accomplishments as a performer and businessperson. According to a member of her management staff, Madonna was upset and worried about what people thought of her: "She knew it was time to make a change. She would have to be pretty stupid not to know it, and you could never say that Madonna was stupid. She was upset, a little frantic about what people were saying about her."[84]

In an effort to call the public's attention back to her work, Madonna spent the mid-1990s and early years of the new millennium reinventing her public image by changing her performance style. At the same time, she transformed her personal life by having two children, exploring new expressions of spirituality, and getting married again.

Reconnecting with Her Audience

In October 1994, Madonna released her tenth album, *Bedtime Stories*, as a step toward softening her public image and reconnecting with her alienated fans. Biographer Mark Bego writes that the new album was still sexy, but in a less confrontational way than *Erotica* had been: "The material found on *Bedtime Stories* was more appealing than that on *Erotica*. Instead of tackling sex head on, this time Madonna is actually sexy in a musically seductive fashion."[85]

Bedtime Stories was a success, and the album's second single, "Take a Bow," became a number one hit, winning Madonna the distinction of earning the most number one hits by a solo female performer. Critical acclaim for the album was also great, and many critics applauded the album for its personal honesty. Jim Farber of *Entertainment Weekly* writes: "More than any previous Madonna album, the latest finds her telling us the truth about her life."[86]

Wearing pajamas, Madonna reads from David Kirk's children's book "Miss Spider's Tea Party" at her Bedtime Stories *performance in 1995.*

A year later, Madonna continued her effort to reconnect with her audience by releasing her eleventh album. Entitled *Something to Remember*, it was a collection of her favorite ballads from 1984 to 1995, and also included three new songs. In the liner notes to the album, Madonna laments that the controversy and negative publicity of her career over the past years had caused her fans to forget her music. She writes: "So much controversy has swirled around my career this past decade that very little attention ever gets paid to my music. The songs are all but forgotten."[87]

Madonna, however, wanted the album to be more than just a greatest hits collection. She also wanted to record the artistic transformation she was experiencing. She had begun her career primarily performing other people's songs, but over the years, she had written more of her own lyrics and music. She felt that her songs had become better and more important as a result. Further, assembling *Something to Remember* was an emotional experience for her because she saw how much she had changed as an artist since her early career. Madonna says:

> Listening to this record took me on my own journey. Each song is like a map of my life. . . . The songs, they choke me up. . . . I can't tell you how painful the idea of singing "Like a Virgin" or "Material Girl" is to me now. I didn't write either of those songs, and I wasn't digging deep then.[88]

Changing Her Public Image

Madonna also wanted the public to see that she was changing her behavior. So, on February 13, 1995, almost a year after her regretted appearance of the previous year, Madonna appeared again on *The Late Show with David Letterman.* She brought Letterman a box of candy and a bouquet of long-stemmed roses as a Valentine's Day gift and to show she was sorry. She apologized for her use of obscenity in her last appearance, and also showed her sense of humor by cursing immediately after she apologized. "I'm a changed woman," she said to the studio cam-

In 1995, Madonna strove to improve her public image.

era. "I'm not going to say f— anymore."[89] The audience and Letterman laughed.

Working Her Way Back in Acting

As Madonna worked to improve her public image, she also wanted to improve the public's perception of her as an actress. After the poor popular and critical reception of her last two films, Madonna said she was interested less in becoming a star than a quality actress: "Obviously I haven't hit my stride in movies, but let me say this: I'm not particularly interested in becoming a great big movie star. I am interested in becoming a good actress."[90]

To begin improving her abilities and rebuilding her reputation as an actress, Madonna took supporting roles in films made by some of the best-regarded directors and stars in the entertainment industry. These parts were so small that many viewers did not know she was in the films until she appeared on screen. In 1995, she appeared in a comedy called *Four Rooms*, playing a witch, Elspeth. The same year, she appeared in *Blue in the Face* as a singing telegram deliverer, and then took a role in director Spike Lee's *Girl 6* (released in 1996) as a struggling actress who takes a job as a phone sex operator. None of the films did well at the box office or won much critical acclaim, but by the end of 1995, Madonna felt she had proven her renewed seriousness about her acting career. Her confidence and credibility growing, she decided to pursue the most important acting role of her life: playing Evita Perón.

Evita

In 1994, director Alan Parker announced he was going to make a film version of the Broadway musical *Evita*. Based on the life of Eva Perón, nicknamed Evita, the film depicts the life story of the charismatic and beloved wife of Argentinean dictator Juan Perón. *Evita* was already a famous and successful stage play, and the lead role in the movie was sought after by numerous actresses, including Michelle Pfieffer and Meryl Streep.

When Madonna heard about the film project, she became very interested. Madonna had studied the life of Eva Perón and identified with her. Like Madonna, Perón was a woman with a strong personality and great ambition who was both beloved and misunderstood by the public. To convince Parker to hire her, Madonna wrote him a letter saying that she was the best person for the role. She says, "I remember . . . writing an impassioned four-page letter to [him], listing the reasons why I was the only one who could portray [Eva Perón], explaining that only I could understand her passion and her pain."[91]

In addition to feeling a kinship with Perón, Madonna also felt she had an advantage over the others interested in the part. *Evita* was a musical, and she was one of the world's most famous singers. Whatever the reason for Parker's decision, he chose Madonna, and she worked to prepare for the role.

Recording *Evita*

Written by the award-winning team of composer Andrew Lloyd Webber and lyricist Tim Rice, *Evita* was a challenging musical. It featured songs that were difficult for even professional singers to perform well because of the musical range and power they required. As experienced a singer as Madonna was, she found the songs very challenging. The musical's most important and most difficult song, "Don't Cry for Me Argentina," was the first one Madonna had to record. She had to sing it in front of Webber and an eighty-four-piece orchestra on the first day of the soundtrack recording.

Even though Madonna had spent weeks taking intensive voice training lessons to prepare, she was still very nervous about performing for Webber. Madonna says, "I was so nervous

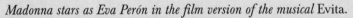

Madonna stars as Eva Perón in the film version of the musical Evita.

because I knew that Andrew had had reservations about me, and here I was singing the hardest song in the piece. All of a sudden there, with everybody for the first time, it was really tense."[92] Her worries proved valid. When the day's recording was over, Madonna was very upset about the quality of her performance. "I was a complete mess," she recalls, "and sobbing afterward. I thought I had done a terrible job."[93] Webber agreed that the performance was substandard. He did not blame her for the problems, however. Instead he fired the orchestra, hired a new conductor, and the recording process went on.

Madonna sings Evita*'s most important and challenging song, "Don't Cry for Me Argentina."*

Giving It Her All

The soundtrack was only the first part of the challenge the film presented for Madonna. Even though she had convinced Parker and Webber that she could portray Evita Perón, many Argentineans were not convinced. Perón was an important figure in Argentina, and there was concern by many that, because of her controversial performances and works, Madonna should not play the role. Even the archbishop of Buenos Aires said, "Madonna is pornographic and unsuitable."[94] But Madonna was determined to play the part. She arranged a meeting with Argentina's president Menem and convinced him that she would portray the national figure with respect and dignity. When Menem's official approval was announced, public criticism subsided and filming began without any problems.

Filming of *Evita* got under way in Buenos Aires in February 1996. Madonna worked hard on the film, studying her role obsessively, rehearsing, and acting in the dust and intense heat of the South American summer. "I was dying from heat exhaustion," she wrote in her diary, "and being made a meal of by ants and flies and hornets."[95]

Parker praised Madonna's professionalism and dedication on the four-month-long film shoot. He says, "Madonna promised me from the very beginning she would give her all, and she has kept her promise."[96] Madonna's costar, Antonio Banderas, also praised Madonna's dedication and said her performance was the best of hers he had seen:

> [She] was absolutely professional. . . . She was so focused, so obsessed with this movie and what it represents to her in terms of her career as well as the personal commitment to this character. . . . She's got pieces of truth in this movie that she's never gotten in even the best video she's done. For the first time—and this is a subjective opinion—she's an actress.[97]

Pregnant!

One of the complications that arose for Madonna during the production of *Evita* was her discovery in March 1996 that she was

Madonna in a scene from Evita. *Madonna maintained a high degree of professionalism throughout production of the film, even after discovering that she was pregnant.*

pregnant. The baby's father was her boyfriend, Carlos Leon, a personal trainer turned actor and model, whom she had met in 1993. With almost three months of filming left, Madonna worried that her pregnancy would alarm director Alan Parker and perhaps jeopardize the film production. However, when she told Parker, he was supportive. He arranged to reschedule the production of much of the movie to accommodate her condition. The cast filmed physically challenging scenes earlier in the schedule so that she would not have difficulty performing them when she gained weight from the baby. He also arranged for Madonna's costumes to be altered to hide the pregnancy as much as possible.

Not wanting to complicate the filming of *Evita* with press attention, Madonna kept the pregnancy a secret from everyone except Leon and Parker until late April. When she did tell others, she called her father first. She then told a journalist she liked, and the journalist published the story.

Some of the first public reactions to Madonna's pregnancy were negative. Many journalists criticized her for not being married to the child's father. In response, Madonna argued that she loved Leon but that they had no plans to marry. She also defended her ability to bring up a child well without being married. "I don't have to get married to have a good relationship and raise children,"[98] she said.

When the filming of Evita was finished, Madonna eagerly awaited the birth of her baby. However, the pregnancy was difficult for Madonna, both physically and psychologically. Backache and fatigue plagued her for several months. Additionally, the pregnancy had been a surprise. Since she had not planned it, she felt slightly out of control, something she was not used to. But she explained that the pregnancy gave her a new perspective and helped her learn to accept being out of control.

Lourdes

On October 14, 1996, after hours of trying natural childbirth techniques, Madonna was taken to a delivery room at Good Samaritan Hospital in Los Angeles for a cesarean section, joking

Marriage

When she became pregnant in 1996, Madonna was criticized by religious groups and members of the press for not wanting to marry the child's father, Carlos Leon. Madonna defended her decision and explained her concerns about marriage in an October 1996 interview, quoted in Barbara Victor's book *Goddess: Inside Madonna*:

> I don't think marriage is a religious thing. It's an economic thing. It's more about money than anything else. It evolved out of women not being able to take care of themselves financially and so having to become a man's possession—promising to love, honor, and obey him. So I don't know what I think of marriage anymore, other than it's an institution which grew out of a very sexist way of thinking and living . . . I don't know what function it could have in my life. If I love someone and want to be with him, there isn't a piece of paper or a ceremony in the world that is going to keep me away from that person. And if I don't want to be with him, the reverse applies. . . . I think marriage is more about what society expects from you than what God does.

as she went. "Goodbye everyone, I'm going to get my nose job now,"[99] she said to family and reporters. Soon after, at 3:30 P.M. doctors delivered her daughter, whom Madonna named Lourdes Maria Ciccone Leon.

Shortly after the birth of Lourdes (nicknamed Lola), Madonna and Carlos Leon ended their nearly four-year relationship. The press and numerous biographers speculated about the cause of the breakup, but neither Madonna nor Leon ever commented on it. Regardless of the cause, says Rosie O'Donnell, Madonna and Leon worked to keep the relationship together but failed. "They made a valiant effort to stay together,"[100] she says.

Madonna carries her newborn daughter Lourdes as the two arrive in Rome for the European premiere of Evita.

Beyond *Evita*

One of Madonna's first public appearances as a new mother was on December 14, 1996, at the premiere of *Evita* at the Shrine Auditorium in Los Angeles. When the film opened a few weeks later, it received predominantly good reviews and made more than $1 million in its first weekend. In January of 1997, Madonna won the Golden Globe Award for best actress for her performance in the film. In her acceptance speech, she spoke about her professional good fortune with the movie and her personal good fortune in the birth of her child, saying "I have been so incredibly blessed this past year."[101] Elsewhere, she acknowledged the role the film played in transforming her life:

> *Evita* was really challenging, an emotionally exhausting and soul-searching couple of years for me. It was a real education, the farthest I've ever had to push myself creatively. It was exhausting and intimidating. I've never been so drained by anything. From the beginning I walked into another world—and kissed the world as I knew it good-bye. Even more important, it was an event that profoundly changed my life and gave me enormous joy.[102]

Although she won the Golden Globe, she did not get an Academy Award nomination, even though many critics and fans thought she deserved one. Despite being overlooked for the nomination, Madonna attended the Oscar ceremony, performing "You Must Love Me," which won the award for best song in a motion picture for Andrew Lloyd Webber and Tim Rice.

Ray of Light

In the years after *Evita*, Madonna turned her attention back to music. In March 1998, she released *Ray of Light*, her first album since the birth of her daughter. Many critics saw *Ray of Light* as an incredible achievement, saying it marked a dramatic change in her music and in her public image.

Soon after Lourdes was born, Madonna had begun studying and exploring various spiritual books, including important texts

Madonna poses with her Golden Globe award for best actress in a musical or comedy for her work in Evita.

of the Jewish, Buddhist, and Hindu religions. As a result, she developed a strong interest in Eastern spiritual beliefs and practices, such as yoga and meditation. These influences had an impact on *Ray of Light.* The lyrics of the album's songs reflected her spiritual inquiries, and she appeared in several of the album's videos wearing traditional Eastern clothing such as saris and togas.

Madonna felt she had been enlightened by her spiritual studies and wanted to share what she had learned through her music. She said:

> This album is reflective of where I am in my life right now—in terms of my musical interests and in terms of my personal beliefs. I feel like I've been enlightened,

and that it's my responsibility to share what I've learned so far with the world.[103]

Guy Ritchie

Madonna's personal transformation took another significant step in 1998 when she met her future husband, Guy Ritchie. Following the birth of her daughter, Madonna spent increasing amounts of time in London, England, working on music and exploring potential film projects. She liked England and felt it was a safer place than America to bring up her daughter.

While in England, Madonna became close friends with the rock musician Sting and his wife Trudi Styler. During a party in 1998, Sting and Styler introduced Madonna to Guy Ritchie, an English director ten years her junior whose first film, *Lock, Stock, and Two Smoking Barrels*, Sting coproduced. Madonna was attracted to Ritchie on meeting him and had a premonition about their future. "I saw my life in fast-forward," she said.

Yoga and Spirituality

During the late 1990s, Madonna began studying Eastern religious and philosophical practices, such as yoga and meditation. She credits the new ideas with transforming her life. In a 1998 interview quoted in Mark Bego's book, *Madonna: Blonde Ambition*, Madonna discussed how her life has changed:

> I totally feel like I'm starting over. . . . I feel like I've grown so much in the past couple of years. It's been an incredible journey. It's like a light got turned on, which is one of the reasons I call [my 1998] album *Ray of Light*. I now realize that fame is not as important as I thought it was . . . I look at everything I've done in the past and just say, "Wow, I accomplished a lot, and there was goodness there and I could see the struggle in my search," but I just feel like I'm looking at life differently now.

> Yoga has definitely changed my outlook on life. . . . Now I feel that yoga is a total metaphor for life. I had this notion that it was going to be easy, but it wasn't. Also, I got really infuriated with my teacher because she would only teach me a little bit every time. And that was a huge lesson for me. . . . If you're in a hurry, you can't embrace or enjoy yoga. So that was a lesson for me—to enjoy the stillness of it.

"[I knew he would be] my future husband and the father of my second child."[104]

Madonna and Ritchie spent the next several months dating, both in England and in the United States. As their relationship became more and more serious, Ritchie encouraged Madonna to move to London permanently so that they could pursue a

Madonna and Guy Ritchie pose for photographers. Madonna met her second husband, Ritchie, at a party in 1998.

Madonna and Ritchie greet the press after baptizing their son, Rocco.

long-term relationship. Madonna was reluctant, however. Although Leon had given Madonna sole custody of their daughter, Madonna had promised him regular visitation with Lourdes. She asked Leon to move to London also, but his acting career was in New York, and he refused. Finally, Madonna promised continued visits, but decided to move to London, knowing she would return to the United States for work.

Rocco

Soon after moving to London, Madonna became pregnant by Ritchie in early 2000. From the start, Madonna was concerned about the pregnancy. Since Lourdes had been delivered by C-section, Madonna worried there might be complications with her second pregnancy as well. The concern proved justified. Late in the evening of August 10, 2000, she was rushed to Cedars Sinai Hospital in Los Angeles, bleeding and in pain.

Madonna performs during her 2001 tour. Now in the third decade of her career as musician and actress, Madonna remains as popular as ever.

Complications with the pregnancy made it necessary for the baby to be delivered immediately by C-section, even though the baby was not due for several weeks. Although born underweight at 5 pounds 9 ounces, her baby, a son, was born healthy on August 11, 2000. Ritchie and Madonna named him Rocco.

Four months following the birth of their son, on December 22, 2000, Madonna and Ritchie married in Scotland. The ceremony was a contrast to her first wedding. Her wedding to Penn had been a frenzied affair, but the wedding to Ritchie, performed in Scotland's Skibo Castle, was private and well guarded. The only public photos of Madonna and Ritchie were taken with their permission after the ceremony.

Madonna in the New Millennium

Madonna's reinvention of her career and transformation of her personal life were complete as she embarked on the third decade of her career. In the first years of the new millennium, she divided her time between family and her career, intertwining the two when possible. In her acting career, she worked with her husband on a new film entitled *Love, Sex, Drugs, and Money*. When filming completed in November 2001, she shifted her attention back to the theatre, returning to stage acting for the first time since 1988. She worked on the play *Up for Grabs*, which premiered in May 2002 at London's Wyndham's Theater.

She also released the album *Music* in 2001 and embarked on her first tour in eight years, the sold-out *Drowned World* tour. Then, in the beginning of 2002, she released her *Greatest Hits Volume 2*.

Since her career began, Madonna has become a world-famous musician, well-known actress, and successful businessperson. She remains one of the most sought-after performers in the world and one of the most recognized celebrities.

Notes

Introduction: The Phenomenon

1. Jancee Dunn, "The Music Woman," *Rolling Stone*, September 28, 2001, p. 31.
2. Quoted in Ingrid Sischy, "Madonna," *Interview*, March 2001, p. 155.

Chapter 1: Getting Attention

3. Quoted in J. Randy Taraborrelli, *Madonna: An Intimate Biography*. New York: Simon & Schuster, 2001, p. 9.
4. Quoted in Robert Hofler, "An Affair to Remember: Madonna Makes Love to the Camera," *Life*, December 1986, p. 50.
5. Quoted in *Teen Magazine*, "Madonna: She's One Lucky Star!," January 1985, p. 39.
6. Quoted in Denise Worrell, "Now: Madonna on Madonna," *Time*, May 27, 1985, p. 78.
7. Quoted in Worrell, "Now," p. 78.
8. Quoted in Worrell, "Now," p. 78.
9. Quoted in Christopher Connelly, "Madonna Goes All the Way," *Rolling Stone*, November 22, 1984, p. 14.
10. Quoted in Carl Wayne Arrington, "Madonna in Bloom," *Time*, May 20, 1991, p. 56.
11. Quoted in Carrie Fisher, "True Confessions: The *Rolling Stone* Interview with Madonna," *Rolling Stone*, June 27, 1991, p. 47.
12. Quoted in Fisher, "True Confessions," p. 45.
13. Quoted in *Ladies Home Journal*, "Madonna Flexes Her Muscles," November 1990, p. 198.

14. Quoted in Taraborrelli, *Madonna: An Intimate Biography*, p. 23.

15. Quoted in Worrell, "Now," p. 78.

16. Quoted in Worrell, "Now," p. 78.

17. Quoted in Liz Smith, "Madonna Grows Up," *Good Housekeeping*, April 2000, p. 104.

18. Quoted in Worrell, "Now" p. 78

19. Quoted in Taraborrelli, *Madonna: An Intimate Biography*, p. 27.

20. Quoted in Andrew Morton, *Madonna*. New York: St. Martin's Press, 2001, p. 56.

21. Quoted in Morton, *Madonna*, p. 57.

22. Quoted in Barbara Victor, *Goddess: Inside Madonna*. New York: HarperCollins, 2001, p. 176.

23. Quoted in Victor, *Goddess*, p. 177.

Chapter 2: Struggle and Sacrifice

24. Quoted in Worrell, "Now," p. 78.

25. Quoted in Gerri Hershey, "Madonna," *Rolling Stone*, November 13, 1997, p. 98.

26. Quoted in Victor, *Goddess*, p. 176.

27. Quoted in Victor, *Goddess*, p. 177.

28. Quoted in Lynn Hirschberg, "The Misfit," *Vanity Fair*, April 1991, p. 200.

29. Quoted in Connelly, "Madonna Goes All the Way," p. 14.

30. Quoted in Morton, *Madonna*, p. 83.

31. Quoted in Taraborrelli, *Madonna: An Intimate Biography*, pp. 70–71.

Chapter 3: New Beginnings

32. Quoted in Taraborrelli, *Madonna: An Intimate Biography*, p. 73.

33. Victor, *Goddess*, p. 254.

34. Quoted in Cable News Network, "People in the News: Madonna Profile," 2001. www.cnn.com

35. Quoted in Morton, *Madonna*, p. 130.

36. Quoted in Guy D. Garcia, "People," *Time*, February 25, 1985, p. 75.

37. Quoted in Taraborrelli, *Madonna: An Intimate Biography*, p. 86.

38. Quoted in James McBride, "Hollywood Sizzle," *People Weekly*, May 13, 1985, p. 40.

39. Quoted in John Skow, "Madonna Rocks the Land: Sassy, Brassy and Beguiling, She Laughs Her Way to Fame," *Time*, May 27, 1985, p. 74.

40. Quoted in Mikal Gilmore, "The Madonna Mystique," *Rolling Stone*, September 10, 1987, p. 36.

41. Quoted in Barbara Victor, *Goddess*, p. 266.

42. Quoted in *People Weekly*, "Madonna," March 11, 1985, p. 112.

43. Quoted in Fred Schruers, "Can't Stop the Girl," *Rolling Stone*, June 5, 1986, p. 28.

44. Quoted in Chris Chase, "Madonna: The Material Girl and How She Grew," *Cosmopolitan*, July 1987, p 133.

45. Quoted in Gilmore, "The Madonna Mystique," p. 36.

46. Quoted in Roger Wolmuth, "Madonna Lands Her Lucky Star," *People Weekly*, September 2, 1985, p. 22.

Chapter 4: Troubles and Triumphs

47. Quoted in Morton, *Madonna*, p. 140.

48. Quoted in Morton, *Madonna*, p. 141.

49. Quoted in Joanne Kaufman, "Everyone Said It Wouldn't Last . . . and It Didn't. Madonna and Sean Go Their Separate Ways," *People Weekly*, December 14, 1987, p. 13.

50. Quoted in Morton, *Madonna*, p. 145.

51. Quoted in Mark Bego, *Madonna: Blonde Ambition*. New York: First Cooper Square Press, 2000, p. 169.

52. Quoted in Kaufman, "Everyone Said It Wouldn't Last . . . and It Didn't," p. 13.

53. Quoted in Morton, *Madonna*, p. 148.

54. Quoted in Taraborrelli, *Madonna: An Intimate Biography*, p. 130.

55. William A. Henry III, "Madonna Comes to Broadway," *Time*, May 16, 1988, p. 98.

56. Quoted in Bego, *Madonna: Blonde Ambition*, p. 206.

57. Quoted in Henry, "Madonna Comes to Broadway," p. 98.

58. Quoted in Bill Zehme, "Madonna: The *Rolling Stone* Interview," *Rolling Stone*, March 23, 1989, p. 50.

Chapter 5: Controversy

59. Madonna, *Like a Prayer*, liner notes, Sire Records, 1989.

60. Quoted in Taraborrelli *Madonna: An Intimate Biography*, p. 161.

61. Quoted in Bego, *Madonna: Blonde Ambition*, p. 223.

62. Bego, *Madonna: Blonde Ambition*, pp. 222.

63. Quoted in Don Winbush, "Bringing Satan to Heel: Tired of Sex and Violence on the Air, the Rev. Donald E. Wildmon Has Discovered the Quickest, Most Effective Route to the Networks' Conscience Is Through Their Pocketbooks," *Time*, June 19, 1989, p. 54.

64. Quoted in Taraborrelli, *Madonna: An Intimate Biography*, p. 168.

65. Quoted in Kevin Sessums, "White Heat," *Vanity Fair*, April 1990, p. 148.

66. Quoted in Brian D. Johnson, "Spanking New Madonna: A Mega-Star Fights Her Way to the Top," *MacLean's*, June 18, 1990, p. 48.

67. Mark Coleman, "'I'm Breathless': New Material for the Material Girl," *Rolling Stone*, June 14, 1990, p. 135.

68. Quoted in Sessums, "White Heat," pp. 148–208.

69. Quoted in Adrian Deevoy, "If You're Going to Reveal Yourself, Reveal Yourself! Madonna Talks Tough About Life and *Truth or Dare*," *Rolling Stone*, June 13, 1991, p. 35.

70. Johnson, "Spanking New Madonna," p. 48.

71. Jay Cocks, "Madonna Draws a Line: After MTV Rejects Her Latest Video, the Material Girl Launches a Program of Self-Defense and Self-Promotion," *Time*, December 17, 1990, p. 74.

72. Cocks, "Madonna Draws a Line," p. 74.

73. Stanley Kauffmann, "*Truth or Dare*," *New Republic*, June 10, 1991, p. 26.

74. Ralph Novak, "*Truth or Dare*," *People Weekly*, May 27, 1991, p. 15.

75. Quoted in Hershey, "Madonna," p. 98.
76. Quoted in Taraborrelli, *Madonna: An Intimate Biography*, p. 228.
77. Taraborrelli, *Madonna: An Intimate Biography*, p. 229.
78. Thom Duffy, "Performance Review: Wembley Stadium, London, September 25, 1993," *Rolling Stone*, November 11, 1993, p. 25.
79. Morton, *Madonna*, p. 231.
80. Taraborrelli, *Madonna: An Intimate Biography*, p. 233.
81. Quoted in Bego, *Madonna: Blonde Ambition*, p. 292.
82. Quoted in Taraborrelli, *Madonna: An Intimate Biography*, p. 234.
83. Quoted in Mary Murphy, "Madonna Confidential," *TV Guide*, April 11–17, 1998, p. 25.

Chapter 6: Reinvention and Self-Discovery

84. Quoted in Taraborrelli, *Madonna: An Intimate Biography*, p. 241.
85. Bego, *Madonna: Blonde Ambition*, p. 293.
86. Jim Farber, "Swinging a New Jack," *Entertainment Weekly*, October 28, 1994, p. 74.
87. Madonna, *Something to Remember* (liner notes), Warner Brothers, 1995.
88. Quoted in Timothy White, "'Something' in the Way She Grieves," *Billboard*, September 30, 1995, p. 5.
89. Quoted in Alan Bash, "Madonna Makes 'Late Night' Peace," *USA Today*, February 14, 1995, p. 3D.
90. Quoted in Denis Ferrara, "Madonna: A Self-Styled Experiment in Sexuality—Her Own Work of Erotic Art," *Cosmopolitan*, February 1996, p. 128.
91. Madonna, "Madonna's Private Diaries," *Vanity Fair*, November 1996, p. 174.
92. Quoted in Richard Zoglin, "Mad for *Evita*," *Time*, January 20, 1997, p. 29.
93. Quoted in Larry Flick, "Radio Embraces *Evita*," *Billboard*, September 30, 1995, p. 1.
94. Quoted in Paul Du Noyer, "Commanding," *Q*, December 1996, p. 26.

95. Quoted in Taraborrelli, *Madonna: An Intimate Biography*, p. 256.

96. Quoted in Julie Salamon, "Madonna's Moment as Evita, Mother, and Fashion Force/Madonna Moment," *Vogue*, October 1996, p. 300.

97. Quoted in Marco R. della Cava, "Bandaras Faces the Music: *Evita* Tests Press-Shy Star's Voice and Mettle," *USA Today*, January 3, 1997, p. 1D.

98. Quoted in Taraborrelli, *Madonna: An Intimate Biography*, p. 275.

99. Quoted in Todd Gold, "Labor of Love: After Twelve Exhausting Hours, Madonna Gives Birth to a Healthy Baby Girl," *People Weekly*, October 28, 1996, p. 48.

100. Quoted in Morton, *Madonna*, p. 222.

101. Quoted in Morton, *Madonna*, p. 221.

102. Quoted in Victor, *Goddess*, pp. 337–338.

103. Quoted in Larry Flick, "WB Expects Madonna to *Light* Up International Markets," *Billboard*, February 21, 1998, p. 1.

104. Quoted in Victor, *Goddess*, p. 352.

Important Dates in the Life of Madonna

1958
Madonna Louise Ciccone is born in Bay City, Michigan, on August 16.

1963
Mother, Madonna Fortin, dies when Madonna is five years old.

1976
Begins studying dance on scholarship at University of Michigan in Ann Arbor, Michigan.

1978
Quits college to move to New York City; studies with Pearl Lang.

1979
Joins band the Breakfast Club after quitting dance.

1982
First single, "Everybody," is released.

1983
Full-length debut album, *Madonna*, is released.

1984
Begins filming *Desperately Seeking Susan*, her first lead role in a feature film, costarring with Rosanna Arquette.

1985
Begins first tour, *The Virgin Tour*, for her second album, *Like a Virgin*; marries actor Sean Penn on her twenty-seventh birthday.

1988

Appears in David Mamet's *Speed-the-Plow*, her first stage role on Broadway; files for divorce from Sean Penn.

1989

Controversial video "Like a Prayer" is released; it later wins 1989 MTV Viewer's Choice Award.

1990

Embarks on controversial *Blonde Ambition* World Tour and films *Truth or Dare* documentary; new video "Justify My Love" banned by MTV for its adult themes.

1992

Releases controversial book *Sex*, which goes on to sell 1.5 million copies.

1996

Begins filming *Evita* in Buenos Aires; daughter Lourdes Maria Ciccone Leon born in Los Angeles.

1997

Wins Golden Globe Award for best actress for appearance in *Evita*.

1999

Moves permanently to London, England.

2000

Gives birth to second child, Rocco Ciccone, in Los Angeles; marries English director Guy Ritchie in Dornoch, Scotland.

2001

Begins *Drowned World* Tour, first tour in eight years; *Greatest Hits Volume 2* is released.

For Further Reading

Books

Nichole Claro, *Madonna*. New York: Chelsea House, 1994. Short juvenile biography on Madonna with good photographs.

Keith Elliot Greenberg, *Madonna*. Minneapolis, Lerner, 1986. Short juvenile biography up through Madonna's early career.

Works Consulted

Books

Mark Bego, *Madonna: Blonde Ambition.* New York: First Cooper Square Press, 2000. Good biography with excellent source notes. Contains a few black and white photographs.

Editors of Rolling Stone, *Madonna: The Rolling Stone Files: The Ultimate Compendium of Interviews, Articles, Facts and Opinions from the Files of* Rolling Stone. New York: Hyperion, 1997. Excellent resource of articles from one of the best periodical sources on Madonna's career. Covers the years 1984 to 1996.

Andrew Morton, *Madonna.* New York: St. Martin's Press, 2001. Good in-depth biography covering Madonna's career through early 2001. Includes many photographs and comprehensive discography and filmography.

J. Randy Taraborrelli, *Madonna: An Intimate Biography.* New York: Simon & Schuster, 2001. Good chronological narrative of Madonna's life and career up to 2000 with good bibliographical information and photographs.

Barbara Victor, *Goddess: Inside Madonna.* New York: HarperCollins, 2001. Lengthy biography with numerous personal anecdotes. Poor bibliographical notes, few photographs (but all in color).

Periodicals

Carl Wayne Arrington, "Madonna in Bloom," *Time,* May 20, 1991.

Alan Bash, "Madonna Makes *Late Night* Peace," *USA Today,* February 14, 1995.

Chris Chase, "Madonna: The Material Girl and How She Grew," *Cosmopolitan*, July 1987.

Jay Cocks, "Madonna Draws a Line: After MTV Rejects Her Latest Video, the Material Girl Launches a Program of Self-Defense and Self-Promotion," *Time*, December 17, 1990.

Mark Coleman, "I'm Breathless: New Material for the Material Girl," *Rolling Stone*, June 14, 1990.

Christopher Connelly, "Madonna Goes All the Way," *Rolling Stone*, November 22, 1984.

Adrian Deevoy, "If You're Going to Reveal Yourself, Reveal Yourself!: Madonna Talks Tough About Life and *Truth or Dare*," *Rolling Stone*, June 13, 1991.

Marco R. della Cava, "Bandaras Faces the Music: *Evita* Tests Press-Shy Star's Voice and Mettle," *USA Today*, January 3, 1997.

Paul Du Noyer, "Commanding," *Q*, December 1996.

Thom Duffy, "Performance Review: Wembley Stadium, London, September 25, 1993," *Rolling Stone*, November 11, 1993.

Jancee Dunn, "The Music Woman," *Rolling Stone*, September 28, 2001.

Jim Farber, "Swinging a New Jack," *Entertainment Weekly*, October 28, 1994.

Denis Ferrara, "Madonna: A Self-Styled Experiment in Sexuality —Her Own Work of Erotic Art," *Cosmopolitan*, February 1996.

Carrie Fisher, "True Confessions: The *Rolling Stone* Interview with Madonna," *Rolling Stone*, June 27, 1991.

Larry Flick, "Radio Embraces *Evita*," *Billboard*, September 30, 1995.

——, "WB Expects Madonna to *Light* Up International Markets," *Billboard*, February 21, 1998.

Guy D. Garcia, "People," *Time*, February 25, 1985.

Mikal Gilmore, "The Madonna Mystique," *Rolling Stone*, September 10, 1987.

Todd Gold, "Labor of Love: After Twelve Exhausting Hours, Madonna Gives Birth to a Healthy Baby Girl," *People Weekly*, October 28, 1996.

William A. Henry III, "Madonna Comes to Broadway," *Time*, May 16, 1988.

Gerri Hershey, "Madonna," *Rolling Stone*, November 13, 1997.

Lynn Hirschberg, "The Misfit," *Vanity Fair*, April 1991.

Robert Hofler, "An Affair to Remember: Madonna Makes Love to the Camera," *Life*, December 1986.

Brian D. Johnson, "Spanking New Madonna: A Mega-Star Fights Her Way to the Top," *MacLean's*, June 18, 1990.

Stanley Kauffmann, "*Truth or Dare* (review)," *New Republic*, June 10, 1991.

Joanne Kaufman, "Everyone Said It Wouldn't Last . . . and It Didn't. Madonna and Sean Go Their Separate Ways," *People Weekly*, December 14, 1987.

Ladies Home Journal, "Madonna Flexes Her Muscles," November 1990.

Madonna, "Madonna's Private Diaries," *Vanity Fair*, November 1996.

James McBride, "Hollywood Sizzle," *People Weekly*, May 13, 1985.

Mary Murphy, "Madonna Confidential," *TV Guide*, April 11–17, 1998.

Ralph Novak, "*Truth or Dare* (review)," *People Weekly*, May 27, 1991.

People Weekly, "Madonna," March 11, 1985.

Julie Salamon, "Hotter Than Furnaces: Exposing Madonna's Maiden Film," *Vanity Fair*, October 15, 1985.

———, "Madonna's Moment as Evita, Mother, and Fashion Force/ Madonna Moment," *Vogue*, October 1996.

Fred Schruers, "Can't Stop the Girl," *Rolling Stone*, June 5, 1986.

Kevin Sessums, "White Heat," *Vanity Fair*, April 1990.

Ingrid Sischy, "Madonna" *Interview*, March 2001.

John Skow, "Madonna Rocks the Land: Sassy, Brassy and Beguiling, She Laughs Her Way to Fame," *Time*, May 27, 1985.

Liz Smith, "Madonna Grows Up," *Good Housekeeping*, April 2000.

Lauren Spencer, "Madonna's First Flop," *Rolling Stone*, October 23, 1986.

Teen Magazine, "Madonna: She's One Lucky Star!," January 1985.

Timothy White, "'Something' in the Way She Grieves," *Billboard*, September 30, 1995.

Don Winbush, "Bringing Satan to Heel: Tired of Sex and Violence on the Air, the Rev. Donald E. Wildmon has Discovered the Quickest, Most Effective Route to the Networks' Conscience Is Through Their Pocketbooks," *Time*, June 19, 1989.

Roger Wolmuth, "Madonna Lands Her Lucky Star," *People Weekly*, September 2, 1985.

Denise Worrell, "Now: Madonna on Madonna," *Time*, May 27, 1985.

Bill Zehme, "Madonna: The *Rolling Stone* Interview," *Rolling Stone*, March 23, 1989.

Richard Zoglin, "Mad for *Evita*," *Time*, January 20, 1997.

Albums

Madonna, *Like a Prayer*. Sire Records, 1989.

Madonna, *Something to Remember*. Warner Brothers, 1995.

Internet Sources

Cable News Network, "People in the News: Madonna Profile," 2001. www.cnn.com. Brief biography with links to a Madonna timeline, video gallery, photo gallery, and Madonna quiz.

Internet Movie Database, "Madonna," 1990–2002. http://us. imdb.com. Comprehensive listing of Madonna's motion picture and television career history as guest, actress, composer, or producer. Also includes a photo gallery and link to Madonna trivia.

Rolling Stone.com, "Madonna," 2002. www.rollingstone.com. Excellent resource, including Madonna articles, biography, message boards, concert files, discography, photos, trivia, and video. Also includes links to album reviews and fan sites.

Index

Picture Credits

About the Author

Andy Koopmans is also the author of *The Importance of Bruce Lee*, and his short stories, poetry, and essays have appeared in journals all over the United States. He lives in Seattle, Washington, with his wife Angela Mihm, dog Zachary, and cats Licorice and Bubz.